OSPREY AVIATION ELITE • 2

56th Fighter Group

SERIES EDITOR: TONY HOLMES

OSPREY AVIATION ELITE • 2

56th Fighter Group

Roger A Freeman

OSPREY
AVIATION

Front cover
In late February 1944 a high pressure period gave clear skies over much of Germany, and allowed the USAAF to carry out an intensive series of bombing raids against the German aircraft industry. Popularly know as 'Big Week', the strong enemy opposition encountered resulted in high claims for VIII Fighter Command escort fighters. For example, on the 24th, when the bombers went to Schweinfurt, Gotha and other targets deep in Germany, a total of 60 Luftwaffe fighters were credited as shot down by P-47s, P-38s and P-51s – the 56th FG's contribution was eight. An A group of 38 P-47s and a B group of 34 were despatched by the 56th to afford penetration support for the bombers. The A Group encountered Fw 190s near Kassel, and Maj James C Stewart, leading the 61st FS formation as the unit's CO, downed one and claimed another as a probable.

Based on the experiences of Stewart during this sortie, Jim Laurier's specially-commissioned cover artwork shows the auxiliary fuel tank of a Focke-Wulf fighter exploding after being hit by the major's fire. At this time the three squadrons that made up the 56th FG – the 61st, 62nd and 63rd – carried red, yellow and blue nose recognition bands, respectively, on their Thunderbolts. A blue-nosed 63rd FS aircraft is the other P-47D depicted in this wintry scene.

Jim Stewart was an original combat member of the 61st FS, and was credited with a total of 10.5 aerial victories, one probable and three damaged. From a flight leader, he rose to command the squadron from 13 January to 13 April 1944, when he completed his operational tour and was transferred to VIII Fighter Command HQ

Back cover
The 61st FS's 2Lt Steve Gerick poses with his crew chief, Sgt Paul Blanford, on 'their' P-47D Thunderbolt, 42-26024/HV-O. This photograph was almost certainly taken near the end of Gerick's tour with the 56th FG (he transferred out on 27 June 1944), for it shows ten kills painted beneath the cockpit of the aircraft. The pilot's final tally was five aerial kills, nine damaged and two destroyed on the ground

First published in Great Britain in 2000 by Osprey Publishing
Elms Court, Chapel Way, Botley, Oxford, OX2 9LP

© 2000 Osprey Publishing Limited

ISBN 1 84176 047 1

Edited by Tony Holmes
Page design by Mark Holt
Cover Artwork by Jim Laurier
Aircraft Profiles by Chris Davey
Origination by Grasmere Digital Imaging, Leeds, UK
Printed through Bookbuilders, Hong Kong

00 01 02 03 04   10 9 8 7 6 5 4 3 2 1

EDITOR'S NOTE
To make this new series as authoritative as possible, the Editor would be interested in hearing from any individual who may have relevant photographs, documentation or first-hand experiences relating to aircrews, and their aircraft, of the various theatres of war. Any material used will be credited to its original source. Please write to Tony Holmes at 10 Prospect Road, Sevenoaks, Kent, TN13 3UA, Great Britain, or by e-mail at tony.holmes@osprey-jets.freeserve.co.uk

For details of all Osprey Publishing titles please contact us at:

Osprey Direct UK, P.O. Box 140, Wellingborough, Northants NN8 4ZA, UK
E-mail: **info@ospreydirect.co.uk**

Osprey Direct USA, P.O. Box 130, Sterling Heights, MI 48311-0130, USA
E-mail: **info@ospreydirectusa.com**

Or visit our website: **www.ospreypublishing.com**

CONTENTS

FORMATION AND TRAINING

n 1942 the United States Eighth Air Force, based in the United Kingdom, began a campaign of strategic bombing against German war industry. Its *modus operandi* was high altitude precision attack by large formations in daylight. The bombers employed, B-17 Flying Fortresses and B-24 Liberators, were heavily armed, and the hope was that they could endure enemy fighter interceptions. It soon became clear that the losses incurred made these raids prohibitive.

The bomber formations desperately needed long-range fighter escorts, but the provision of such aircraft with the performance (and the necessary endurance) to match the enemy initially proved most problematic. The desired range capability was eventually forthcoming, most notably through the introduction of the Rolls-Royce Merlin-powered P-51 Mustang, which could range anywhere the bombers went. Moreover, in affording protection for the bombers the American fighters eventually attained air supremacy in enemy airspace – an achievement that proved a major contribution to Allied victory in western Europe.

The main protective force involved was that of VIII Fighter Command, whose principal commander, Brigadier General William Kepner, commented that while the P-51 Mustang was the aircraft that dealt the

When initially formed at Savannah, Georgia, in January 1941, all the 56th PG had in the way of mobile equipment was a few battered Army trucks. The group's first aircraft (again in similar condition to this suitably-decorated Dodge T215 WC26 'half-tonner') would not arrive for another five months. Posing proudly alongside his 'charge' is the 61st PS's Sgt Elois Dauphin

Lt Gene O'Neill of the 62nd PS is seen preparing for a flight in one of the few P-38Es operated by the 56th at Bendix Airport in April 1942. At this time the group expected to be equipped with the Lockheed fighter. Having joined the 56th PG just prior to Christmas 1941, O'Neill remained with the 62nd PS/FS through until the completion of his tour on 20 February 1944. By this time he had accumulated 200 hours of combat flying and downed 4.5 aircraft – post-war, he has often been credited with five victories, although the former score is given both in the USAF's Historical Study 85 and the VIII Fighter Command's Final Assessment. Aside from his aerial victories, O'Neill also returned home with the Silver Star, three Distinguished Flying Crosses (DFC) and four Air Medals

Luftwaffe the *coup de grâce*, it was the P-47 Thunderbolt that broke its back. Indeed, it was P-47 units, before the arrival of the P-51, that took on the best of the *Jagdverband*, and brought attrition from which the Luftwaffe in the west never recovered.

Foremost of the Thunderbolt equipped units was the 56th FG which, despite being the only one of 15 Eighth Air Force fighter groups not to convert to the longer-ranged Mustang before the end of hostilities, was credited with more enemy aircraft shot down than any of the other USAAF fighter groups flying in Europe. The two most successful USAAF fighter aces were members of the group, and there were many others who distinguished themselves. But above all, it was the 56th's developed fighting spirit that 'showed the way' to other Eighth Air Force fighter groups.

'Constituted' (which meant that authorisation had been granted to form and designate a new fighter organisation) on 20 November 1940, the 56th Pursuit Group (PG) was to be composed of a headquarters and three new pursuit squadrons, namely the 61st, 62nd and 63rd. It got no further than being a paper reference for the next seven weeks, but on 14 January 1941 the 56th was given physical existence with orders for activation. Three officers and 150 enlisted men from units at Hunter Field, Georgia, were duly assigned to the National Guard building in nearby Savannah. Other personnel were subsequently posted in, but it was not until May 1941, following a move to Charlotte Army Air Base in North Carolina, that the neophyte organisation was brought to life as a flying unit – albeit only with a few training aircraft and three well-worn P-39 Airacobras and five P-40 Warhawks.

The demand for military aircraft was such that the squadrons could not muster a dozen fighters apiece until transferring to South Carolina following the Japanese attack on Pearl Harbor and the United States' entry into World War 2. Here, the three squadrons were placed on different airfields, and given obsolete P-36s to bolster aircraft complements. The stay was short, for in January 1942 the 56th PG was selected to provide an air defence for New York, despite the fact that it was unlikely that any defence would be required for a city located so far from air hostilities. Here, the squadrons were again placed on three different airfields, and their aircraft complements increased with the inclusion of a few P-38s Lightnings and more P-40 Warhawks. By April 1942 production allowed the group's full re-equipment with P-40Fs. Personnel strength had also been gradually built up, and while some men were moved on to other recently-formed units, by the spring of 1942 the group was near to its authorised complement of 800 men, of which 80 were pilots.

While the group headquarters was located in an army installation at Teaneck, New Jersey, the 61st PS took up station at the Bridgeport airport in Connecticut, the 62nd at Bendix airport, New Jersey, and the 63rd on an airstrip serving the Republic Aviation Corporation at Farmingdale on Long Island, New York.

Republic was just commencing production of its new P-47B Thunderbolt fighter which, unlike most of its contemporaries, employed an air-cooled radial engine in the shape of the recently-developed Pratt & Whitney R-2800, developing 2000 hp. Designed as a high-altitude interceptor, the P-47 featured turbo-supercharging for the engine, which gave it top speeds in excess of 400 mph at the then very high altitudes of 25,000 to 30,000 ft. In comparison with the P-39 and P-40, the P-47 was a giant both in size and weight.

With part of the 56th PG deployed on Republic's doorstep, it came as no surprise when, in May 1942, the group was selected to be the first outfit in the army air force to equip with the new type – the first example was received the following month. Also in May the USAAF discarded the term 'pursuit', all units so identified thus being re-designated as 'fighter'.

The changes continued throughout the summer of 1942, as the USAAF altered the structure of its combat groups by disbanding headquarters squadrons. Thereafter, a group headquarters was a slimmed down organisation providing the united administration and leadership for three combat squadrons. During July and August this brought some reorganisation of personnel within the 56th, and the concentration of all elements in Connecticut, the Headquarters, 61st and 63rd FSs at Bridgeport, where facilities had been extended, and the 62nd on a new military airfield at Windsor Locks. Col John Crosswaithe assumed command at this time, but was replaced in September by Maj Hubert Zemke.

Already boasting considerable flying experience on the Curtiss P-40, Zemke had been sent to Britain in the spring of 1941 to advise on the handling of the Curtiss fighters acquired by the RAF, which had named them Tomahawks. Soon after Zemke's arrival, Hitler made his attack on the Soviet Union, and in an immediate gesture of help, the British shipped many of the Tomahawks on to Russia. Zemke and another US officer followed with a small party of RAF mechanics to help the Russians with assembly, Zemke acting as test pilot. On return to the US his experience warranted command of a fighter group being groomed for overseas duty.

Through the summer and autumn of 1942 the 56th accelerated its training on the Thunderbolt. In practice it became a test unit on the type for Republic, whose engineers closely monitored usage. Numerous modifications were made as a result of unsatisfactory reports made by 56th pilots and engineers. Some of the early problems encountered by the group included the distortion of the P-47B's fabric-covered rudder and ailerons and the fracturing of its wooden radio mast when the aircraft was subjected to high-speed manoeuvring. Other incidents also occurred, although these were not generally the fault of the aircraft. Several eager, but relatively inexperienced, pilots not long from training establishments failed to observe due caution and suffered a series of accidents. Indeed, only a few of these could be blamed on weaknesses in the aircraft.

The 56th FG soon found that if the P-47's rate of climb was not impressive, its high altitude performance was, and at 30,000 ft runs at 400 mph were easily obtained – speeds equal or better to any fighters the enemy or Allies then had in service. However, dives from altitude needed caution, and at least two of the group's pilots were killed when they failed to recover. Compressibility was the probable cause, a phenomena about which little was know at the time.

On 13 November 1942, two 63rd FS pilots, Lts Harold Comstock and Roger Dyar, flying new P-47C models which featured metal-covered rudders and elevators, encountered compressibility in high altitude dives which produced unprecedented speeds – probably in the region of 500 mph. Republic publicity took advantage of this incident to proclaim the two P-47s had come near to the speed of sound.

In late November the group was alerted for overseas movement, and its P-47Bs and early Cs were passed to other units. The USAAF had decided to establish two P-47-equipped fighter groups in the UK to support its daylight bomber operations, and the 56th would be one of these. The other was already in England, and would convert from Spitfires. In the event, another group in England, which had its P-38s and pilots transferred to North Africa to make up losses, also re-equipped with P-47s.

After a month of awaiting orders to move, the 56th's personnel travelled by train to Camp Kilmer, the embarkation holding post at New Brunswick. After a week of so-called processing, the group sailed on the *Queen Elizabeth* in the early hours of 6 January 1943 in company with some 11,000 other US servicemen, including those of the 33rd Service Group, which would provide the engineering back-up for the 56th in the ETO (European Theatre of Operations).

A flight of 61st FS P-47Bs is led over Long Island Sound in September 1942 by the 56th FG's newly-arrived CO, Maj Hubert Zemke. Denoting its assignment to the latter pilot, 41-6002 has three stripes (in squadron colours of red, yellow and blue) encircling the rear fuselage, and a nose cowling band also similarly decorated. This aircraft was damaged in an accident on 10 October 1942, and after repair went to Westover Field, Massachusetts, on 20 November. It was finally written off in an accident on 14 January 1943

KING'S CLIFFE AND HORSHAM

The 56th FG's Atlantic crossing proved to be both swift and uneventful, and the group disembarked at Gourock, in the Clyde estuary, on 12 January 1943 – just six days after leaving Camp Kilmer. The men then completed their posting to the ETO with a slow train journey to King's Cliffe, in England's east midlands. Here, Headquarters and the 61st and 62nd FSs were settled in on the nearby local airfield, while the 63rd was trucked the short distance to RAF Wittering.

The latter unit quickly settled into the creature comforts on offer at an established RAF airfield, which boasted barrack blocks. However, for the bulk of the 56th FG, cold winter weather soon exposed the inadequacies of the hutted accommodation at Wittering's satellite site at King's Cliffe.

Press Day for the Thunderbolt, King's Cliffe, 10 March 1942. Lt Robert Stultz of the 62nd FS poses for size contrast on the cowling of P-47C 41-6209. The Pratt & Whitney R-2800 Double Wasp it housed was one of the most powerful, and hardy, radial engines ever built. This P-47, coded LM-V, was shot down on 30 July 1943, while Stultz fell victim to the Luftwaffe on 17 August that same year

Although the 56th was the first group to fly the P-47, and its pilots were highly proficient in handling the type, two weeks passed before the first example was received at King's Cliffe. This led to some frustration within the group, for it was known that P-47Cs (the first combat model) had arrived in the UK shortly before the New Year. Despite the 56th's experience, the first examples available were sent to the 4th FG, whose pilots were not impressed with the big fighter. Indeed, they openly stated that they would have preferred to have kept their more nimble Spitfires.

These early P-47Cs also suffered their fair share of technical problems too, the most troublesome of which was caused by the replacement of the factory-fitted medium frequency radios with the vitally necessary very high frequency models. Communication with the new equipment proved virtually impossible due to noise intrusion, and this was not cured until much work had been carried out on suppressing leaks from the engine's electrical system. This delayed giving the Thunderbolt operational status until early April when, in preparation, the 56th moved all units to Horsham St Faith, in Norfolk, on the 5th of that month.

Like Wittering, Horsham St Faith was a so-called permanent RAF station with brick-built buildings and comfortable accommodation. In addition to the near 1000 men assigned to the 56th FG, there were some 750 in the service and support units which made up the complete complement gathered at this station on the outskirts of the City of Norwich. The airfield was grass-surfaced, and had been used by RAF light bomber squadrons for operations during the first three years of the war. The sod surface allowed flights of four P-47s to take off together, line abreast.

Although assigned to VIII Fighter Command, the American fighter force at first operated under RAF Fighter Command operational control.

This flight of 61st FS P-47Cs was photographed on a training sortie near Wakerley on 10 March 1943. At this time the group was in the process of applying white identity bands to its Thunderbolts and outlining the fuselage National Insignia in yellow – indeed, only the second aircraft in the formation exhibits both. The lead Thunderbolt, later named *Doc* (eight other aircraft in the squadron were named after Disney *Snow White* characters), was flown by Capt Don Renwick. P-47C 41-6267 was assigned to Lt Joe Powers, whilst 41-6261 – one of the first two Thunderbolts received by the group on 24 January 1943 – was later transferred to the 63rd FS. The last fighter in this loose line up is 41-6325, which was assigned to Lt Robert Johnson

Operational procedures employed were as developed and practised by the more experienced command, and it was vital that all Allied forces conformed to these. Operational initiation came on 8 April when Col Zemke, Maj David Schilling and Capts John McClure and Eugene O'Neill in aircraft of the 62nd FS joined a combined formation of 4th and 78th FG P-47s for a high altitude sweep of the Pas de Calais area of the French coast.

The experienced 4th FG, the successor of the RAF's 'Eagle' Squadrons, led what the term sweep suggests – a brief brush through hostile airspace. The official code name for a sweep was 'Rodeo', and its object was to bring up enemy fighters to battle, although the Luftwaffe usually only challenged these intrusions when in a position of advantage. Five days later Zemke took the same pilots in another four-fighter flight with a formation from the other groups on a second uneventful sweep over enemy territory.

Later the same day a four-aeroplane flight from each of the 61st and 63rd FSs joined Zemke with the 62nd flight for a combined sweep by the three groups. This time some anti-aircraft artillery fire was observed below but again no enemy aircraft were seen. Capt Roger Dyar experienced engine failure during the course of the mission, and was fortunate in having enough altitude to keep control and regain the English coast, 'bellying in' near Deal. Dyar's P-47 had suffered a blown cylinder head, which was suspected to have been caused by over-boosting. Similar failures were experienced with other P-47s over the following weeks, and the problem was eventually cured by the installation of an interconnected control adjustment for both the throttle and turbo-supercharger.

On 15 April another sweep was flown, this time with the 24 aircraft put up by the 56th operating by themselves, rather than as part of a larger formation with another group. Two more sweeps during the next few days were also uneventful, apart from mechanical or equipment failures which

Notable visitors were often received by the group, including Herbert Lehman, Director of the US Office of Foreign Relief and former New York Governor. He came to Horsham St Faith in the spring of 1943 to see an operational P-47 group to which his son, then undergoing a theatre indoctrination course, was expected to be assigned. However, rather than joining the 56th FG, Flt Off Peter Lehman was assigned to the 4th FG's 336th FS (in late August 1943) instead. He subsequently lost his life on 21 March 1944 when his P-51B Mustang flicked over and spun into the ground near Duxford during a low-level mock dogfighting sortie. Walking along the flightline with Herbert Lehman are, from left to right, Lt Conway Saux, who was killed in an air collision, Lt Mike Quirk, who amassed 12 air victories before becoming a PoW after flak crippled his aircraft in September 1944, and Lt Harry Coronios, killed on a training flight in November 1943. The party is walking towards Quirk's aircraft, whose Donald Duck insignia is partially visible in the top right hand corner of the photograph

Photographed from the Horsham St Faith control tower, these eight 62nd FS Thunderbolts were lined up for the press on 26 April 1943. The nearest aircraft is Lt Ralph Johnson's *PUD*, and parked beside it is Capt John McClure's 41-6394/LM-M. Three days after this photograph was taken, McClure and his Thunderbolt became one of the first two losses sustained by the 56th FG – McClure survived as a PoW. Group, squadron and flight leaders often had the initial letter of their surname as the individual letter of their aircraft's code marking, although in some cases it was the initial letter of their first, or popular, name

This 61st FS P-47C was also photographed at Horsham St Faith on 26 April 1943. Standard USAAF positioning of the National Insignia on the wings was upper surface on the left and lower surface right. Because of the common belief that any fighter with a radial engine must be an Fw 190, an over-size National Insignia was added to the underside of P-47 right wings in the UK

caused aborts (the term for abandoning an operational flight through such circumstances).

These sweeps continued to be unchallenged by the Luftwaffe until 29 April. Continuing the programme of gaining operational experience for the P-47 pilots, over 100 aircraft were sent on high level sweeps on this date, the 56th being tasked with overflying the Dutch and Belgian coastal areas. Leading the group for the first time was the CO of the 62nd FS, Maj Dave Schilling.

During the flight Schilling's radio failed, but instead of handing over to another pilot and returning home, he continued to lead. As the formation started to withdraw, the 62nd was 'bounced' from above by Fw 190s. In the brief action which followed, the P-47s of Schilling's wingman, Lt Winston Garth, and Capt John McClure were shot down. Both pilots were, however, able to use their parachutes, bailing out into captivity. Schilling's P-47 and that of another 62nd pilot received battle damage.

On return to Horsham St Faith, Schilling was all for taking off again to do battle with the enemy. Calmed by Zemke, he was later admonished by the group CO for not handing over leadership of the formation when his radio failed. It was evident that air discipline needed improvement, and the exuberant 'buddy-buddy' atmosphere that existed amongst pilots needed an injection of sobriety. Zemke realised that he had to become more the disciplinarian at the risk of unpopularity. Always something of a loner with ambitions for his command, the forceful Zemke never attained

Capt 'Doc' Renwick, 1Lt 'Norm' Brooks and Capt 'Gabby' Gabreski of the 61st FS are seen in conversation at Horsham St Faith on 26 April 1943. Renwick eventually became the last CO of the 56th while in England. Gabreski wears RAF flying boots, which were preferred by many US fighter pilots in the ETO

Ten of the original combat pilots of the 61st FS pose in front of Lt Milton Anderson's P-47C 41-6237/HV-A *THE IDAHO SPUD* during the 26 April 1943 press call. They are, standing left to right, Don Renwick, Merle Eby, Norman Brooks, Dick Mudge and Leslie Smith. Squatting, left to right, Joseph Powers, Kirby Tracy, Francis Gabreski, Loren McCollom and Joseph Curtis. Of these, Eby and Tracy were killed, and Gabreski, McCollom and Mudge were made PoWs. Gabreski and Smith became squadron commanders, and Renwick the group commander. Finally, Smith, Gabreski and Powers also attained ace status with the 56th FG

the popularity that Dave Schilling enjoyed. Personable and easy going, if impulsive and sometimes given to be uncautioned, Schilling was the star personality of the group. Loren McCollom and Phillip Tukey, the 61st and 63rd FS commanders', were by contrast less exuberant.

The code name for an escort or bomber support was 'Ramrod', and on 13 May the 56th was given its first, providing cover for B-17s attacking the Luftwaffe airfields near St Omer. This was uneventful, but next day a similar task met strong opposition determined to attack the bombers. A number of diving interceptions brought claims of a probably destroyed enemy and two damaged, although once again inexperience in ranging was apparent and air discipline was still lacking with some pilots.

The group was despatched on another 13 missions during May 1943, usually flying three squadron formations of 12 aircraft. However, squadron strength was being raised to 25 aircraft, which allowed each squadron to put up 16 aircraft apiece on 29 May. Thereafter, this would be the desired norm for a mission, with three flights of four in trail and stacked down below the leader's four-aeroplane flight. In hostile airspace each flight opened up for battle formation, with about 500 yards between each aircraft. On the last day of May the group suffered another loss over enemy-held territory when 1Lt Pat Williams' Thunderbolt went into an uncontrolled dive from which it never recovered. Failure of the oxygen system was the suspected cause of this tragedy.

In compliance with an VIII Fighter Command directive, in early June Col Zemke selected Loren McCollom to be his deputy and Flying Executive Officer. He had long considered McCollom the most able and practised of his squadron commanders. Capt Francis Gabreski, who had the most operational experience in the 61st FS, replaced McCollom as its commander. Gabreski, a Polish American, had been sent on detachment from the group to fly Spitfires with one of the RAF's Polish-manned squadrons, and the operational experience he gained during this brief time away was most welcomed by the 56th FG upon his return in March 1943.

The Rodeo flown on 12 June resulted in the first credit for an enemy aircraft destroyed by the group. While over Belgium, and with the advantage of being up sun, the 62nd FS found itself in the position to make diving attacks on a *Staffel* of Fw 190s seen several thousand feet below. Maj Schilling took his flight down but overshot. A second flight was more successful, and its leader, Capt Walter Cook, fired at 300 yards and saw pieces fly from the wing of an Fw 190 before it went into an uncontrollable spin. The next day would prove to be even more fruitful.

A formation of Fw 190s was seen some 10,000 ft below the Thunderbolts, and Zemke led two flights down to intercept. The enemy flight selected for attack apparently did not see the P-47s approaching for the group CO shot down two and 2Lt Robert Johnson was credited with destroying another. However, Johnson's success was tempered by his breaking away from his flight without permission – the second such occasion he had done this during combat. Much as he admired Johnson's aggressiveness, Zemke could not condone this breach of air discipline, and the errant pilot was duly admonished.

This pattern of operations continued through June, the group flying mostly Rodeos and the occasional close escort for B-17s attacking targets within the P-47's radius of action. The average duration of these missions was one-and-a-half hours, of which some 30 minutes was spent over enemy-occupied territory. The climb to 30,000 ft, and the necessity for high speed in hostile airspace, saw the P-47's 305-US gallon fuel load consumed at a rate averaging 200 gallons an hour. Under full power in combat, this figure rose to near 300 gallons an hour – the R-2800 had a prodigious appetite.

The most well known photographs of 56th FG Thunderbolts are those taken by the press from a B-24 on 25 May 1943. This echelon down is led by 62nd FS Operations Officer Capt Horace Craig in his P-47D 42-7870/LM-R *PAPPY*. Next is P-47C 41-6264/LM-X *TWO ROLL CHARLIE*, which *was* assigned to Lt Conway Saux, then Capt O'Neill's P-47C 41-6347/LM-O *LIL ABNER*, followed by Lt Robert Taylor's P-47C 41-6193/LM-B *GINGER*, Lt Robert Stover's P-47C 41-6209/LM-C, and Lt Harry Coronios' P-47D 42-7860 *GREK*. Only Craig and O'Neill would survive hostilities

To extend its range when operating over France, the group often flew to an RAF station on the south coast to replenish fuel tanks before setting out on a mission. Such was the case on 26 June 1943 when Manston, in Kent, was the forward base used.

Led by the 56th's Flying Executive, Maj McCollom, 49 P-47s took off

---

COMBAT REPORT

What follows is Col Hubert Zemke's personal report on the Ramrod flown on the morning of 22 June 1943. The encounter with an Fw 190 took place from 28,000 ft down to 5000 ft, with thin cirrus at very high altitude and a few low alto-cumulus. Visibility was 15 to 20 miles;

'I was leading the 56th Fighter Group. On this operation the fighters of the USAAF were late to their rendezvous with the bombers through no fault of their own. Each Wing Commander knew this, so the original plan of a column of squadrons for each individual group was disregarded. As a result all ran into each other in the vicinity of the bombers, causing a complex situation of identification and battle.

'As leader of the first squadron of the 56th Group, I headed for a formation of unidentified fighters close to the rear of the bombers and prepared for action. This attack was head-on through a group of P-47s of another Group, not enemy aircraft, and as a result split my lead squadron up into pairs and flights. After two more attacks on planes which were later identified as P-47s, I saw an aircraft below and at least five miles away which was pressing an attack on the rear of the bomber formation. An attack was pressed on this aircraft, but because of the distance the rate of closure did not enable me to spring a surprise attack. The enemy aircraft recovered by pulling upwards just as I launched my attack from above. At this point each of us identified the other. The enemy broke in a left circle just as I was closing on him, causing me to give a 30-degree deflection shot for three seconds. My added speed enabled me to gain a bit more altitude then he, although my circle was much wider.

'The next attack was about 45 degrees from the front, and as we closed the enemy aircraft went into an aileron roll of about two turns straight down. I followed, but on recovery, I found that both the enemy aircraft and myself were recovering up at an angle of 45 degrees, each endeavouring to gain an altitude advantage over the other. As was the case, he

finally levelled off with an altitude advantage of about 2000ft. The enemy aircraft position was then at eight o'clock to me. My only alternative was to turn into him in a chandelle. His attack on me, therefore, was a dive which carried him past me. As he went past I reversed direction to follow his dive but, due to my slow acceleration – whereas he was diving – I could only give a burst with long range deflection.

'We again circled and recovered altitude, with the enemy aircraft on top by 2000 or 3000 ft, going in the same direction and out to the side, the altitude by now being close to 10,000 ft. Again my only choice was to bear in on a head-on attack in order to shake him as much as possible. He continued on through the head-on, and as he passed me I would let a burst go and then turn and try to follow him down.

'This last dive carried us to 5000 ft, where he began a very slight climbing turn. My ammunition ran out as I fired at a range of 400 yards with a deflection of a ring-and-a-half.

'The engagement was immediately broken off and I turned away from him to go into a shallow dive towards home, passing out of enemy occupied territory between Schowen and Walchern Island. On looking back I noticed that the enemy aircraft was in a similar dive going towards Flushing and was not endeavouring to press home an attack. Both of us were probably out of ammunition and were satisfied that we had had all the combat we wanted for one day.

'Points that were learned on my part were that the Fw 190's recovery and climb were superior to mine from the time I lost my initial altitude advantage. His ability to gain altitude in a circle was definite, and the only alternative when he dived was to come as close as possible to ramming him head-on before he circles too many times and got on my tail.

'The entire combat was extremely interesting, and makes me a confirmed dive-and-recovery artist in the future, especially at low altitudes.'

A gallery of 63rd FS pilots and their assigned aircraft, as photographed on 25 May 1943

Capt Lyle Adrianse with his P-47C 41-6362/UN-A *Michigan Mauler*. Flight B commander, Adrianse shot down two enemy aircraft during his tour. His P-47C was retired to serve with the 495th Fighter Training Group (FTG) in September 1943

Lt Jack D Brown straddles the cockpit of his P-47C 41-6203/UN-J *WINDY*. His Crew Chief, S/Sgt Hoyette Redding, stands at the wing root, and his assistant, Cpl George Sakakeeny, is by the wheel. *WINDY* was another P-47C passed to the 495th FTG in September 1943

Lt Wayne O'Connor with dog 'Slipstream' on his P-47C 41-6216/UN-O, which boasted a big bad wolf insignia. The aircraft was lost with another pilot on 19 August 1943, whilst O'Connor was shot down and killed on 11 November 1943

Lt Joseph Egan poses with his P-47C 41-6584/UN-E *HOLY JOE*. This aircraft was written off after a crash-landing on 1 December 1943, and Egan (a five-victory ace) was killed when his P-47D-25 (42-26524) was shot down by flak near Nancy on 19 July 1944. He had just returned to the ETO to start his second tour, having been promoted to lead the 63rd FS. Egan's command of the unit lasted just 48 hours

Below
63rd FS CO, Maj Philip Tukey, poses with his personal P-47C 41-6375/ UN-T. Tukey went to VIII Fighter Command HQ as an operations officer at the end of September 1943, and was later given command of the 356th FG at Martlesham Heath. The Thunderbolt in this photograph was crash-landed at Eastchurch on 2 September 1943 by Lt John Vogt after being severely savaged by an Fw 190

at 1812 hours tasked to provide withdrawal support for B-17s that had bombed an air depot at Villecoublay, near Paris. Two 63rd FS pilots had to abort due to mechanical trouble before the group made landfall over the enemy coast at Dieppe at between 24,000 and 26,000 ft, 35 minutes after take-off. The bombers were met six minutes latter in the vicinity of Forges and seen to be under heavy attack by numerous Bf 109s and Fw 190s. The P-47s did not have an altitude advantage, and were soon engaged by enemy fighters concentrating attacks on the 61st FS, flying at 24,000 ft.

During the following 20 minutes of air fighting, squadron formations became dispersed, and when returnees were counted, it was apparent that the 56th had had the worst of the encounters. The 61st FS aircraft flown

by 2Lts Justus Foster and Robert Johnson limped back to Hawkinge and Manston respectively, both with extensive battle damage caused by 20 mm cannon shells. The P-47s of 2Lts Eaves (62nd FS) and Clamp (63rd FS) also landed at Manston with 20 mm battle damage, the latter pilot still with a metal fragment lodged in his left arm.

1Lt Ralph Johnson's aircraft, also hit by 20 mm shells, had the hydraulic system holed, causing one wheel to come down. The pilot made for his home station, from where Col Zemke took off to fly alongside and offer radioed advice on manoeuvres to try and shake down the other main wheel leg, which refused to budge. A one-wheel landing would most likely precipitate a fatal crash, and as this leg could not be retracted, Zemke advised Johnson to fly to the coast and bail out over the water. Successfully vacating the cockpit, Johnson's parachute deposited him in the sea just north of Great Yarmouth, where an RAF Air-Sea Rescue (ASR) launch quickly rescued him. But four pilots never returned, three from the 61st and one from the 63rd, all later notified as killed.

On the credit side, only two claims for enemy aircraft destroyed were confirmed – Fw 190s for a third pilot by the name of Johnson, Capt Gerald W, whose gun camera film showed this pilot's skill in aim and range assessment.

Interrogation revealed a confused situation with lack of co-ordination between squadrons. Once again air discipline left much to be desired. As combats had taken place near the same level as the bombers, many of the group's pilots had been forced into slow turning and climbing actions. It

Opposite top
P-47C 41-6537/UN-Q was the mount Lt Wilfred Van Abel, who subsequently went missing in this aircraft on 2 September 1943, although he survived as a prisoner. Crew Chief Sgt Damon Itza, standing on the wing, was selected to look after 'Hub' Zemke's Thunderbolt when the CO moved it from the 62nd to the 63rd FS in September 1943

P-47D 42-7975/UN-C cavorts over Norfolk on 25 May 1943. A few days later this aircraft had its individual 'plane-in-squadron' letter changed to I. The 56th FG did not use the letter C from June to December 1943 in line with the original British Air Ministry recommendations on the use of code letters. Assigned to 2Lt Raymond Petty, UN-I suffered a runaway propeller and engine fire over Holland on 7 November 1943, causing its pilot, Flt Off Robert Sheehan, to bail out. Helped by the Dutch underground movement, he became the first member of the group to evade capture, being returned to England 11 weeks later

The wreckage of P-47D 42-7946/UN-I lays in a Dutch wheat field on 31 May 1943. 1Lt Pat Williams was killed when this aircraft went into an uncontrolled dive from 30,000 ft. The most likely cause of this accident was that the pilot was rendered unconsciousness through lack of oxygen, probably due to a faulty oxygen regulator. The 56th's first operational casualty was given a military funeral two days later

This low pass over Horsham St Faith by Capt Don Goodfleisch in P-47D 42-7878/UN-G and Lt Gordon Batdorf in P-47C 41-6261/UN-B was captured on film on 25 May 1943. Both pilots survived hostilities, Goodfleisch completing a second tour and commanding the squadron. Batdorf was never presented with the opportunity to shoot down an enemy aircraft, and Goodfleisch claimed just two aerial victories in more than 300 hours of operational flying. As the combat records of these two veteran P-47 pilots prove, you had to be in the right place at the right time to become an ace . . .

. . . and Capt Walter Cook certainly was, for he not only shot down the first enemy aircraft claimed by the 56th FG (on 12 June 1943), he also went on to achieve ace status with a further five kills

was clear the P-47 was no match for the Bf 109 or Fw 190 in such circumstances, and this led to Zemke complaining to his superiors that the group's combat effectiveness was hampered by having a fighter with such a poor rate of climb.

The 56th's record up to this time was the least creditable of VIII Fighter Command's three Thunderbolt groups, but the trouncing of 26 June produced a more determined atmosphere amongst the group's personnel. Some pilots harboured revenge, but any who had doubted the Luftwaffe's prowess now took a much more serious view of their task. Zemke's leadership became more severe, which did not endear him to many of his pilots. New formations and tactics were experimented with during the operations of early July, but it was clear that altitude advantage was the key to success with the Thunderbolt.

Slow to accelerate, the P-47 could gain on both the Bf 109 and Fw 190 in a long dive, and an accurately aimed short burst from its eight 0.50-cal guns had a devastating effect on the enemy. The momentum of the dive could be used to zoom-climb back to higher altitude. Slow turning fights were a no go in a combat situation when high speed must be maintained.

HALESWORTH

On 21 June 1943 the 56th had received notice that it was to move from Horsham St Faith to Halesworth, in Suffolk – a move that was far from popular. Horsham St Faith was about to be given concrete runways and facilities to transform it into a heavy bomber station. Halesworth, a new airfield built for heavy bombers, was to be a temporary base for the 56th, with another move in prospect when the site was wanted for occupancy by a bomber group. Many of the domestic sites were not completed and only one of the two scheduled hangars had been erected.

Accommodation was in prefabricated buildings (mostly Nissen huts), whereas Horsham St Faith had brick-built permanent centrally-heated barracks. The one advantage of Halesworth was that it was only five miles from the coast, and thus would slightly extend penetration. The move was made during the opening week of July, and the first group operational mission from the new station was performed on the 10th. Eighteen missions were flown before the group again saw major action.

On 30 July withdrawal support was given to B-17s that had bombed Kassel. Bf 109s were bounced, with credits of five destroyed for two Thunderbolts that failed to return. On this day the 78th FG equipped its P-47s with ferry tanks to extend the fighters' range to the German/Dutch border, thus catching enemy fighters off guard. These were rated as having a capacity of 200 US gallons, but were only partly filled for this mission.

A 20 mm shell strike crippled the hydraulic system and mutilated a flap on Lt Justus Foster's 41-6220/HV-O during the air battle of 26 June 1943. Foster managed to fly the P-47C back to England for a wheels-up crash-landing at Hawkinge, on the Kent coast. This photograph was taken after the Thunderbolt had been lifted and its undercarriage extended

Ranking American World War 1 fighter ace Eddie Rickenbaker visited Halesworth on the afternoon of 28 July 1943 in company with VIII Fighter Command CG, Brig-Gen 'Monk' Hunter (centre). They are seen watching a Thunderbolt fly-by with Col Zemke from the dais used to address an assembled audience of 56th FG personnel. Zemke had led a Ramrod in the morning, and subsequently led another after the guests had departed

The 56th used 'bathtub' ferrying tanks on four missions during August 1943. They proved somewhat troublesome, prone to leaking and sometimes failed to release. Standing ready on a Halesworth hardstanding, *The Flying Ute* was the P-47C assigned to Lt Jack Brown, who came from Utah. This was additional, later decor to the name *WINDY*. Note the playing card painted onto the starboard wheel cover of this aircraft – this was a favourite location amongst groundcrews when it came to personalising their charges

The 56th's first opportunity to use these large bulbous, bathtub-shaped tanks, fitting closely under the fuselage of the P-47, was on 12 August. Unfortunately they were only suitable for low and medium altitude operation, for they lacked a means of pressurisation. Fuel could not be drawn much over 20,000 ft, which meant that the tanks had to be released before reaching the P-47's usual operational altitude. Moreover, the tanks were difficult to install, tended to leak, affected the centre of gravity of the aircraft and sometimes failed to release.

Their use on this occasion enabled the group to be airborne for 2 hours and 12 minutes, giving some 20 minutes of extra cover for B-17s bound for the Ruhr. No successful contact was made on this mission, or on the next two occasions when use was made of the troublesome tanks, but on 17 August the extra duration they provided gave the 56th the opportunity it had been seeking.

This day was famous for the first shuttle raid undertaken by Eighth Air Force bombers, which successfully struck the Regensburg Messerschmitt factory, before flying on to land in Africa. 17 August also marked the first occasion that the Schweinfurt ball-bearing works was struck, a second force of bombers being sent to attack this well-defended target. Finally, this date proved infamous for the loss of 60 B-17s during these operations.

Pappy' Craig commanded the 62nd Fighter Squadron from mid-August 1943 to early the following February. His only confirmed success in air combat was on 20 December 1943 when he shot down a Do 217 bomber

The 56th flew two missions. The first saw P-47s covering the bombers making for Regensburg, and although some interceptions of enemy aircraft took place, there were conclusive results. The second was to meet the B-17s returning from Schweinfurt. With the extended range provided by the auxiliary tanks, the group formations penetrated some 15 miles beyond Eupen to find the bombers heavily engaged with enemy fighters. Most of the enemy aircraft were at the same level as the bombers, orbiting some miles ahead or behind their quarries to reform before launching another attack. This gave the P-47s the advantage of being able to initiate diving attacks on the enemy aircraft before they reached the bombers.

Many Luftwaffe fighters appeared to be taken off guard, probably not expecting the P-47s to be so far inland. Claims of 17 enemy fighters shot down were made as a result of this action for the loss of three P-47s. Two of the successful pilots – 1Lt Glen Schiltz and Capt Gerald Johnson – were credited with three victories each. Two days later the group was able to use similar tactics to claim another nine victories, with the single victory credited to Gerald Johnson making him the 56th's first ace.

To honour this, and further build group morale, Zemke approved a red lining for Johnson's flight jacket. The intention was that all pilots reaching ace status would have this mark of distinction. However, later reassessment

Twenty-five-year-old Capt Gerald W Johnson was proclaimed the first ace of the 56th FG. Considered one of his most able pilots by Zemke, Gerry Johnson eventually amassed a total of 16.5 aerial victories before being shot down by ground fire and made prisoner. In later years he rose to the rank of lieutenant-general in the USAF, and commanded the Eighth Air Force during the Vietnam war. The "*JACKSON COUNTY. MICHIGAN. FIGHTER*" (42-7877/ HV-D) was one of several P-47s received by the 56th carrying acknowledgements to communities or organisations that had raised the fighter's purchase price in war bonds. When Gerry Johnson was detached to fly with the 356th FG in November 1943, 42-7877 reverted to being a pool aircraft until Flt Off Evan McMinn (who later became a five-kill ace) had it assigned to him early in the New Year. At least ten enemy aircraft fell to the guns of this Thunderbolt

Although to the untrained eye this may appear to be just a white blob in an over-exposed frame from a gun camera film, it was enough to bring a destroyed credit for Capt Gerry Johnson on 19 August 1943. This victory (a Bf 109, downed near Gilze-Rijen) made Johnson the 56th FG's first official ace

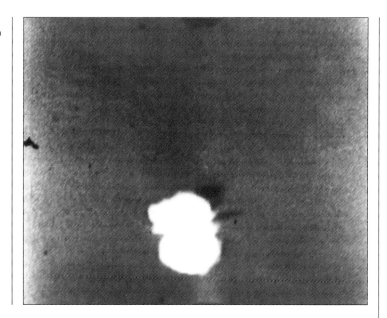

An unofficial aid to inter-flight recognition was the white tail tip on 2Lt Frank McCauley's P-47C 41-6271/ HV-Z *Rat Racer*. This photograph was taken on 24 August 1943 after he had brought the fighter back to Halesworth with a 20 mm cannon shell hole in the left wing. McCauley's assigned fighter, he used *Rat Racer* to claim all 5.5 kills (as well as a probable and a damaged) credited to him during his 46-mission tour

of the claims made on 17 August resulted in one of Johnson's victories that day being shared with another pilot who had attacked the same Bf 110.

In early August the 56th had an additional task – acting as chaperone and mentor to the newly-arrived 353rd FG, based at nearby Metfield. On 16 August the 353rd's CO, Lt Col Joe Morris, became the group's first combat loss when he failed to return from a mission. Soon after 'Hub' Zemke received a 'phone call from Maj-Gen William Kepner, who had recently relieved Gen 'Monk' Hunter in command of VIII Fighter Command. Kepner informed Zemke that he was to send Loren McCollom over to Metfield to become the new CO of the 353rd. Although he had to comply with the order, Zemke was not pleased. The 56th had made great strides towards becoming an efficient and polished team in which McCollom, who alternated mission leads with Zemke, played an important role.

'Mac' went to Metfield the next day and shot down an enemy fighter on his first mission with his new command. Zemke appointed David Schilling as his new deputy, and made Horace Craig CO of the 62nd FS. Late the following month Zemke was to lose another of the original squadron commanders when Philip Tukey was ordered to VIII Fighter Command, where an experienced combat commander was required to act as an Operations Officer. Sylvester Burke in turn took over the 63rd FS.

In the last week of September civilian mechanics arrived to install B-7 bomb shackles under the 'bellies' of the P-47s one squadron at a time, starting with the 62nd. The shackles were to be the means of holding 75-US gallon auxiliary metal fuel tanks which had originally been produced for extending the ferrying range of fighters, notably the Bell Airacobra.

The experimental station at Bovingdon had devised a means of pressurising these teardrop shaped tanks using the exhaust of the P-47's instrument vacuum pump. Pressurisation enabled fuel to be drawn at high altitude, allowing the tank to be retained and only jettisoned if involved in combat action. This was a great improvement over the 200-gallon unpressurised tanks and did not have such a detrimental effect on handling and performance. The first operational use of 75-gallon 'drop tanks' was made on 31 August when Schilling led 36 P-47s on an uneventful Ramrod.

On average the tanks added another half-hour to the P-47's endurance on an operational mission, but with careful engine control endurance

Mechanics work on the engine of Maj Dave Schilling's assigned P-47D 42-7938/LM-S during the afternoon of 3 September 1943 after 'Hub' Zemke had collected a little battle damage in it whilst leading two missions on this day. When an assigned aircraft was out of service for repair, maintenance or modification, the pilot, if scheduled to fly, was allocated another squadron aircraft. Group HQ officers usually took the assigned aircraft of another HQ officer. 'Pappy' Craig's LM-R can be seen in the background of this photograph near the farmhouse dubbed 'Schilling's Acres' by the 56th FG. This building was used primarily by the 62nd FS

Failure to remove the rudder lock prior to take-off resulted in 1Lt Wayne O'Connor being unable to maintain directional control of P-47D 42-22534/UN-O, which ended up in a boundary hedge at Halesworth. The pilot escaped unhurt, but the Thunderbolt was a write-off. This incident occurred on 7 September 1943

Lt William Janson collected some flak fragments in the engine cowling of P-47C 41-6268/UN-P on 22 September 1943. One of the 63rd's first replacement pilots, Janson was assigned this aircraft when Pete Dade was taken off flying to become group Operations Officer

While training in preparation for deployment to the ETO 'Hub' Zemke's P-47B was crewed by the 61st FS. Once in combat, his P-47C 41-6330 was first crewed by the 62nd as LM-Z, and then on 21 September 1943 he moved it to the 63rd, where it became UN-S. This photograph was taken two days later after the aircraft had collected a bullet hole through air ducting in the cowling

could be spun out to as much as two-and-a-half hours. On 27 September, when the bombers raided Emden, the group was airborne for two hours and forty minutes. Cylindrical metal 108-US gallon capacity tanks made in the UK then became available, and these allowed endurances of three hours and penetration well into German airspace.

On 2 October the 56th claimed three enemy aircraft, one of which fell to the guns of 'Hub' Zemke, making him the group's second ace, although due to reassessment he was actually the first. Group and squadron leaders always had more opportunity to shoot down the enemy simply because they headed squadron formations. The term 'ace' was a completely unofficial tag, and came from the French in World War 1, who adjudged a pilot who had shot down five of the enemy to be worthy of this accolade. Zemke was more interested in his group's success than his own, and began to encourage a rivalry with other groups.

Tactics were his absorbing interest, and these were varied without word to VIII Fighter Command. When the B-17s went to Frankfurt on 4 October the 56th provided part of the penetration escort. A formation of twin-engined Bf 110s were spotted preparing to attack the rear Fortress formations near Duren. Led by Schilling, the 63rd FS fell on the enemy, shooting down 14 Messerschmitt heavy fighters – a record score for a USAAF squadron up to that point in the war. The total credited to the group was 16, with Walker Mahurin and Vance Ludwig each being responsible for three.

Four days later another five victories were obtained, and on 10 October 56th pilots were credited with ten kills and on the 14th another three. The first fortnight of October 1943 was an infamous period for VIII Bomber

Command, with 167 B-17s missing in action, whereas in beating off their Luftwaffe tormentors, the 56th had raised its total of victories to 88 – 15 more than the 4th FG, which had been operational for a year.

The 56th's ascendancy led to Zemke, much against his will, being selected to return to America to participate in briefing the Army Air Forces' hierarchy, and those of import, on Eighth Air Force fighter activities. However, he managed to elicit a promise from Gen Kepner that he could return to the UK and continue to command the 56th. To further

P-47D 42-8525/UN-J was the second Thunderbolt assigned to Jack D Brown, and he used it to achieve his only air victory – a Bf 110 – on 4 October 1943

Capt Bob Lamb was not scheduled to fly on 8 October, so 2Lt Gordon Blake (a recent replacement) took Lamb's P-47C 41-6211/HV-L out and duly collected bullet holes in the wings. Lamb was also stood down on 1 December 1943 when the aircraft was shot down. Its pilot on this occasion, 1Lt Cleve Brown, bailed out and was made a PoW. Posing alongside the aircraft in this 8 October photograph is 41-6211's crew chief, S/Sgt Houston

The air fighting on 8 October 1943 gave the 56th five destroyed credits for one loss. Capt Ray Dauphin's P-47D 42-8614/LM-D sustained 20 mm and 7.9 mm hits, one shell entering the right side of the cockpit and shattering instrument glass. Dauphin was slightly wounded by splinters

ensure this he managed to have Col Robert Landry assigned to the 56th as its commander during his absence.

Thirty-four-year-old Landry had been serving as a staff officer at VIII Fighter Command, and was eager to fly combat missions. In Zemke's absence, the day-to-day operational leadership of the group would very much depend on the experienced officers under Dave Schilling.

During the later part of October Zemke had been away from Halesworth making a documentary on VIII Fighter Command P-47 operations to take with him to America. While at 'Ajax' (code name for VIII Fighter Command HQ at Watford), waiting to leave for the US, Zemke learned that a bomber mission was scheduled for 5 November. He was determined to participate in one more mission, and flew to Halesworth to lead the 56th – much to the annoyance of Schilling, who was to have led. It proved to be a fruitful mission, for the group scored six victories without loss to take its total score to 100. The 56th was the first Eighth Air Force fighter group to reach the century mark.

Some weeks earlier the pilots had set themselves the task of claiming their 100th victory by Sadie Hawkin's Day. This was 6 November, and the day when girls were allowed to wed the man of their choice in the popular 'Li'l Abner' syndicated cartoon strip which was featured in the *Stars and Stripes* newspaper. Having achieved their goal, the pilots staged an Officer's Club celebration at Halesworth, which further helped to boost morale within the 56th FG.

COMBAT REPORT

During the Ramrod of 11 November 1943, 2Lt Melvin C Wood's P-47D-2 (42-22478/HV-W) was shot up by a Bf 109 in a surprise attack over Horstmer, Germany. Wood's account gives details of the damage sustained, and the tense experience that followed. 'HG' refers to the measurement of manifold pressure, which reflected the boost input from the turbo-supercharger;

'Attacks were made from 90 degrees following around to dead astern. First strike was a 20 mm cannon shell directly in the centre of the engine cowling on the right side at 90 degrees. The shell exploded in the engine, striking the manifold and oil lines, etc. Fired from 15 degrees dead astern, at least one 20 mm cannon shell entered the fuselage immediately below the right elevator or stabiliser and exploded. Many fragments damaged the bulkheads and other internal parts and one piece came out of the other side in the vicinity of the tail wheel door. Two blades of the propeller were hit by 20 mm cannon shells. One pierced a blade about eight inches from the tip and made a clean hole $1^1/_2$ inches in diameter. This strike evidently came from dead astern. The other blade was damaged for a length of about ten inches, with the entire edge of the blade for four inches in width and ten inches long either torn off or the few remaining edges bent or twisted. This strike could

have been from either 90 degrees or from dead astern.

'When first hit the airplane jumped and bucked and the engine stopped. As I was in a vertical dive the engine started again but was coughing and spitting and running very rough. I proceeded to the deck at about Enschade, and flew from there to about ten miles out into the channel on the deck, drawing $54^1/_2$ inches of mercury and 2720 RPMs. The engine was very rough, coughed a lot and cut out an estimated 40 times, but always momentarily. As I reached mid-Channel I cut it back to 30 HG and 2000 RPMs. The engine was much rougher and the vibration intense. Finally, I had to cut it back to 23 HG and 1400 RPMs. At this speed the vibration was so intense that the pitot tube was vibrating an arc of approximately one foot and the instrument panel four inches. It was impossible to read any of the instruments and I expected the engine to disengage itself from the aircraft at any time. About ten miles from the coast the engine stopped completely when I changed gas tanks, and I finally got it started by priming, turning the emergency fuel pressure clear on and engaging the starter. I landed at my home base with only a couple gallons of gas.

Melvin Wood later lost his life during the Korean War.

The achievements of the 56th also featured regularly in the *Stars and Stripes*, where, because use of unit designations was forbidden, it was referred to as the Zemke Group. Such publicity also helped build pride. A situation was arising where the score in shooting down enemy aircraft was hailed in much the same manner as that in a ball game. For the young pilots involved it was a far more serious business.

The installation of shackles on the Thunderbolts to allow drop tanks to be carried also opened the way for the self-same shackles to be used for bombs – the purpose for which they were originally designed. The first operational use of the 56th's P-47s with bombs took place on 25 November 1943 when 53 fighters set off to rendezvous with a Liberator for a formation drop from 24,000 ft on St Omer/Longuenesse airfield. Although the procedure had been practised over ranges in England, there were problems with timing and formating on the B-24 with the result that most bombs were spread over a wide area beyond the airfield target.

On the same day the neighbouring 353rd FG undertook the first dive-bombing mission with P-47s, and this offered far more promise. Next day the 56th despatched 51 P-47s at 1052 hours to provide withdrawal support for the 'heavies' which had raided Bremen. Carrying 108-US gallon

Maj David Schilling sits in the cockpit of his P-47D 42-7938/LM-S prior to leading the successful mission of 10 October 1943, when he destroyed his fifth aircraft. He is seen talking with his crew chief, S/Sgt Jack Hollznan, prior to engine start

Don Goodfleisch's *Lil Goody* (P-47D 42-7878/UN-G) came to grief after an engine failure on a local flight on 16 October 1943 forced the pilot to perform a belly landing. The personal insignia carried on the engine cowling of 56th FG Thunderbolts often reflected the assigned pilot's nickname. In addition, it was also common practice to have a wife's or girlfriend's name on the fuselage below the cockpit. Sometimes there was another girl's name on the other side of the fuselage too! *Lil Goody* is seen here being investigated by an inquisitive youngster

P-47D 42-74620/HV-B takes off from Halesworth on a local flight. This was the assigned aircraft of Lt Edward Kruer, who joined the 56th in July 1943. Kruer was lost in a collision over the North Sea while flying another aircraft on 11 December 1943. Steve Gerick (who later became an ace, scoring exactly five kills) took over 42-74620 when he arrived in the squadron that same month

Having survived the rudder lock incident at Halesworth on 7 September, 1Lt Wayne O'Connor's luck ran out on 11 November 1943 when he is believed to have been the victim of enemy fighters. This photograph shows Luftwaffe personnel examining the wreckage of his P-47D (42-75722/UN-O) at the crash site near Goesfeld

tanks, the Thunderbolts were able to push their range out to within a few miles of Bremen, where Fortresses were found under attack from Bf 110s and Me 410s (then identified as Me 210s). The vulnerable twin-engined fighters had top cover of Bf 109s, but these were engaging P-38 Lightnings at this time.

Using the dive, fire and recover tactics the 56th shot down 23 enemy aircraft, plus three probably destroyed and nine claimed as damaged. The 62nd FS was credited with 15 of this total, while six pilots each shot down two and Walker Mahurin got three. This was the second occasion

Mahurin had shot down three enemy aircraft during a mission, and this latest 'bag' made him the first Eighth Air Force fighter pilot to take his score into double figures. Several P-47s were damaged by return fire from Bf 110 and Me 410 rear gunners, whilst 1Lt Byron Morrill was forced to bail out after his fuel tank was badly holed. Quickly captured and made prisoner, he was the sole 56th FG loss.

To restrict the range of the P-47s the Luftwaffe adopted the tactic of spirited, if limited, interceptions to force drop tanks to be discarded early into the escort mission. This was tried soon after the 56th penetrated hostile airspace on 11 December, when Bf 109s at *Staffel* strength initiated bounces from way above the group's altitude. The fighters were soon observed and intercepted exclusively by the 62nd FS, leaving the rest of the 56th FG to continue on to rendezvous with the bombers. Once again twin-engined fighters were surprised over Germany, a dozen being shot down and still more damaged. The total credits for the mission amounted to 17, with the only losses being suffered following a collision between two P-47s during combat.

Capt Robert Lamb and 1Lts Paul Conger and Donovan Smith each destroyed three aircraft, although one of Smith's was shared with another pilot. Col Landry claimed a Bf 109, which would prove to be his only vic-

On 26 November 1943 the 56th FG initially claimed 26 aircraft destroyed – then its highest single-day tally of the war. Seen in the post-mission walk down the Halesworth perimeter track for the benefit of the cameraman are, from left to right, Capt W V Cook (2 Bf 110s), Lt S B Morrill (1 Bf 109), Lt J P Bryant (1 Bf 110), Lt J H Truluck (1 Bf 109 and 1 Bf 110), Capt Walker Mahurin (3 Bf 110s), Lt Harold Comstock (1 Bf 110 and 2 damaged), Lt Col David Schilling (2 Fw 190s destroyed and 2 damaged), Maj Francis Gabreski (2 Bf 110s), Maj M C Craig (1 Bf 110 and 1 Me 210), Maj J C Stewart (1 Do 217), Flt Off F W Klibbe (1 Bf 109), Lt Jack Brown (1 Bf 109), Capt E W O'Neill (1 Bf 110 and 1 Fw 190), Lt Raymond Petty (1 Fw 190), Lt I F Valento (3 Bf 110s) and Lt A Carcione (1 Fw 190)

The only loss on 26 November 1943 was 1Lt Byron Morrill, one of the original combat pilots of the 62nd FS. His P-47D 42-7979/LM-I was holed in the fuel tank, and the subsequent loss of gasoline was so great that he was forced to bail out over Holland, where he was quickly captured upon landing. Photographed some weeks prior to his demise, Morrill is demonstrating the early type oxygen mask worn by Thunderbolt pilots in the ETO

tory while commanding the 56th. After this action the Luftwaffe was more cautious in the deployment of their vulnerable twin-engined *Zestören*.

With the build up of Allied fighter strength the Luftwaffe endeavoured to deliver its main interception of Eighth Air Force bombers beyond the range of their escort. With P-51B Mustangs now appearing on the scene this became increasingly difficult, although for the P-47-equipped units range remained a critical issue. Indeed, this was often pushed to the limit, with the result that aircraft sometimes returned with no more than ten to twenty gallons of fuel in their tanks.

Pilots relax and engage in a little 'hangar flying' in the 61st FS Ready Room at Halesworth in the wake of the epic battles of 26 November 1943. Flt Off Frank Klibbe demonstrates how he shot down a Bf 109 on his very first combat mission – he would go on to claim a further six kills during his 63-mission tour. Looking on are Maj Francis Gabreski, who downed two Bf 110s, and Lt Eugene Barnum

Near one for 'Gabby' – Maj Gabreski holds a 20 mm cannon shell that lodged in his engine without exploding during the 26 November mission

COMBAT REPORT

The radio transmissions of fighter pilots on combat missions were monitored by listening stations in England, and transcripts prepared and disseminated accordingly. The following extract covers radio transmissions for the Ramrod of 11 December 1943. Fifty 56th FG P-47s left Halesworth at 1047, and the first break in radio silence was at 1119 hours. Six aircraft were abortive, two were lost in a collision and three suffered battle damage.

The transcript mostly covers the problems encountered by the 63rd FS when it came to jettisoning drop tanks upon penetrating enemy airspace, the interception of the leading 62nd FS, that unit's reforming after the battle, and the return of the other units low on fuel. Atmospheric conditions, distance and other factors meant that not all transmissions were received and recorded, particularly the opening identifications. Note that some pilots called others by name and not the call sign, which was a breach of radio conduct. The action involving the 63rd and 61st FSs was too distant for radio reception. Claims were 17 destroyed and five damaged.

The normal 16-aeroplane squadron formation used by the 56th FG was made up of four four-fighter flights – White, Red, Blue and Yellow, in that order. Two flights made a section, which was distinguished by the leading flight, White or Blue. The flight leader and his No 2 composed the lead element of a flight, and No 3 the leader of the second element, with No 4 as his wingman.

Opposite are the abbreviations, code words and pilot identification for the transmissions.

YS - Yardstick, mission leader Lt Col Schilling
KW - Keyworth, 61st FS
WF - Woodfire, 62nd FS
PG - Postgate, 63rd FS
W - White Flight
R - Red Flight
B - Blue Flight
Y - Yellow Flight
Numerals 2, 3 & 4 - aircraft within the flights
L - Leader of Flight or Squadron
Track Line - 65th Fighter Wing Control
Sturdy - Direction Finding Station
Pills - Fuel
Ha, Ha, Ha - crossing coast
Angels - height
Bogies - unidentified aircraft
Babies - drop tanks
Little Friends - friendly fighters
Big Friends - bombers

KW30 - Gabreski
KW31 - Lamb
KW58 - Powers
PGWL - Landry
PGBL - Burke
PGRL - Vogt
PGR2 - Ross
PGB3 - Comstock
PGR4 - Cavello
PGB4 - Dade
KWR4 - Marangello

From	To	Time	Message
-	-	1119	Woodfire Red 4 needs a spare.
YS	-	1133	Roger, thank you.
PGL	YS	1134	Contrails two o'clock just below you.
YS	PLG	1134	Roger. I can't see them. Keep your eye on them.
-	-	1134	How far out are they?
-	-	1134	About three of them.
-	-	1135	They are quite a ways out.
PGB4	-	1136	Either out of gas or belly tank is not feeding.
-	PGB4	1136	Okay, take it home. How does the rest of your gas look? Is it your belly tank?
PGB4	-	1136	It will feed about ten seconds then quit.
-	PGB4	1136	It is probably a little low. How are your other pills. Okay?
PGB4	-	1136	Okay.
-	PGB4	1136	You better take it home. Can you make it okay?

From	To	Time	Message
PGB4	-	1136	Roger.
YS	-	1137	Any idea of angels? Any angels on them?
YS	-	1137	Okay.
YS	-	1139	Okay, we will go into battle formation.
PGBL	-	1139	Many little friends directly behind us.
YS	-	1140	Okay. Okay, thank you.
PGR2	PGRL	1142	My belly tank is about empty.
PGRL	PGR2	1142	That is about the right time.
YS	PGL	1142	Are you still on tank?
PGBL	YS	1142	I am still on tank.
PGL	YS	1142	On tank.
PGR4	PGBL	1144	My cockpit is smoking, I will have to go back.
PGBL	PGR4	1144	Go back and take a wingman.
PGR4	PGR3	1144	Are you going back with me?
PGBL	PGR4	1144	Take Red 2 back with you.
PGRL	PGR2	1144	Did you get the message? Go back with R4.
PGR2	PGRL	1144	Roger.
PGBL	YS	1145	Baby gone.
PGR2	PGR4	1145	I am behind you. Would you slow down a little bit.
PGRL	PGR3	1146	What is your position?
PGR3	PGRL	1146	I am with another squadron. I will pick you up in a few minutes.
PGBL	-	1147	I will have to ask you to look out above while we drop our babies.
-	PGR4	1148	Make a 360 so I can catch you.
PGB3	PGBL	1148	I will have to return. I can't get this damn tank off.
PGL	YS	1149	Look at 3 o'clock below you. It looks like bogies.
YS	PGL	1149	Those are little friends.
YS	-	1151	Ha! Ha! Ha!
KWR4	-	1153	Big friends at 9 o'clock at 31,000.
YS	-	1154	Okay, I will give them a ring.
PGL	YS	1154	Contrails at one o'clock high to you.
YS	-	1155	Okay you guys get ready. Let's step it up.
PGBL	-	1155	Step it up. Step it up.
-	YS	1155	Do you have those contrails in sight?
YS	-	1155	That is right.
-	-	1156	Here they come.
-	-	1156	Break it right!
Pappy	-	1156	Circle in back. Tell me when to break.
Goody	-	1156	I think we better get on up.
-	B	1156	Make a turn left Blue Flight.
PGL	-	1157	Contrails coming in at 7 o'clock to us.
PGL	YS	1157	Are you continuing on?
YS	-	1157	We are all engaged over here. Let's get in this and chase these bastards out of here.
-	-	1157	Contrails above and 8 o'clock.
-	Pappy	1158	I have a 109 right above me Pappy.
-	-	1158	Break it right.
-	-	1158	Watch that guy, he is going up on us.
-	-	1159	Okay, let's head out on course.
KWL	YS	1159	Are you going on to the bombers?
-	-	1200	109 on your tail somebody!
-	-	1201	There is a 47 up there. Get that God damn 190!
YS	-	1201	Okay, let's try and get ahead of the big friends.
YS	-	1201	Let's try and rendezvous over this little white island.
-	Kelly	1202	See these two coming in at 6 o'clock Kelly?

FROM	TO	TIME	MESSAGE
Kelly	-	1202	I see them. We will have to break them in a minute.
YS	-	1202	One crossed over in front of me but I can't get him.
YS	-	1203	Get to the rendezvous point as quickly as you can.
-	-	1203	Watch those ships coming back down there.
KWBL	-	1204	I have them in sight.
-	-	1204	There is a 190 on a 47's tail: you better break.
-	-	1204	Better break 47.
YS	-	1204	Turning right.
-	-	1204	Come back here, we are in trouble.
-	-	1205	Somebody come back here and help us.
-	-	1206	Let's go get a couple.
-	YS	1207	Which way are you headed now?
YS	-	1208	I am right over this island with white sand all around it at 31,000 ft.
YS	-	1209	Orbiting left over this little island.
-	-	1209	That 47 has got the upper hand down there.
YS	-	1210	Setting course to rendezvous point. We have to get over there.
-	-	1210	I have only 15 pills left. I am going home.
-	-	1210	My engine is running rough, I better go home.
YS	-	1211	Let's go over to the big friends. Does anyone see the big friends?
-	Kelly	1211	They are 47's. Kelly watch them.
YS	-	1212	Anyone under 17 pills go on home. Rather hang around here and see if we can do a little patrol work.
YS	-	1213	We will stay around here. We haven't got enough to stay around.
-	Kelly	1213	How are your pills Kelly?
Kelly	-	1213	Okay, boy.
-	-	1213	Little friends at 9 o'clock and low.
YS	Track Line	1214	We will not be able to make rendezvous. We see some little friends coming in. Tell them we are friendly. We are going to hang around a little bit and hold them off.
YS	-	1215	Do you have plenty of gas?
-	YS	1215	Yes, I got plenty.
-	YS	1217	There are a couple behind you Dave.
YS	-	1217	I see them.
YS	Quirk	1217	What is your position on me?
Quirk	YS	1218	I am about 8 o'clock to you.
-	-	1218	One bogie at 8 o'clock to us.
-	-	1219	Is that a 47 right in front of us?
-	-	1220	Roger.
YS	Quirk	1220	See if we can pick up some business down there.
-	LMU	1226	LMU are you still behind me?
-	-	1226	There are two down there in front of us.
-	-	1227	I think they are friends.
YS	-	1227	There is something high about 8 o'clock.
KWL	YS	1228	Are you with the big friends?
-	Pappy	1229	Are you on your way out?
-	-	1229	How are your pills?
-	-	1229	About 13 1/2.
YS	-	1230	Okay boys, let's break it off.
PGY4	-	1234	I am going down with Brownie.
-	Goody	1235	Hello Goody. Do you see those two contrails over there at 9 o'clock?

FROM	TO	TIME	MESSAGE	FROM	TO	TIME	MESSAGE
-	PGBL	1236	Are you getting along okay?	YS	Sturdy	1252	1-2-3-4-4-3-2-1
-	Nick	1239	You know where you are going Nick?	Sturdy	YS	1252	Steer 300.
Nick	-	1239	No.	KW31	KW30	1254	Hello Gabby. Are you all right?
-	PGL	1239	Two at 3 o'clock to you Postgate Leader.	KW31	Track Line	1254	KW30 is too low to receive.
-	-	1240	You go down. I will cover you.	-	-	1257	My ear hurts like hell.
YS	Burke	1244	I am right behind you and a little to the right.	-	PGWL	1257	Contrail at 9 o'clock.
-	-	1246	I got about ten pills.	KW31	KW30	1258	Hello Keyworth 30. How are you doing?
YS	Reeder	1246	Is that you on my wing?	-	PGW4	1258	How are your pills?
-	-	1247	Let's go home. Let's break it off.	KW31	Track Line	1301	Either Keyworth 30 is too low or out.
-	Gabby	1249	Roger. What part of the coast Gabby? I am there too.	PG36	Sturdy	1308	1-2-3-4-4-3-2-1
KW31	Track Line	1251	Keyworth 31 calling for Keyworth 30. Keyworth 30 is down pretty low overcoast. He had only five pills. Can you call him for a fix?	Sturdy	PG36	1308	Steer 180
				-	-	1308	Are you sure this is England?
				KW53	Sturdy	1311	I am all shot up and I have oil all over the windshield.
PGRL	PGL	1251	Bogie 9 o'clock same level.	Sturdy	KW53	1311	Okay, we will have the crash truck waiting.
				-	Johnson	1314	Take it a little slow coming down, Johnson.

There were a number of instances of P-47s running out of fuel before finding an airfield and having to crash-land. Additional shackles on pylons were becoming available for installation under each wing, allowing two drop tanks to be carried. However, the carrying of two drop tanks did not come into use until May 1944, as the limiting factor with range was the internal fuel supply – enough had to be retained for the return flight after drop tanks had been released. The wing shackles were not popular, as they had a detrimental effect on performance and handling. At this time a wide metal 150-US gallon capacity drop tank was being fabricated in the UK specially for use on P-47 'belly' shackles. These came into use in mid-January 1944 and soon became the preferred type.

A further aid to the performance of the P-47 was the introduction of wide blade propellers, popularly known as paddle blades, which improved high altitude operation. The later Pratt & Whitney R-2800 engines had provision for water injection, and the necessary equipment to provide this was scheduled for installation. Water injection into the combustion chambers allowed high manifold pressure, boosting horsepower. With the paddle blade propeller and water injection, top speed and rate of climb were significantly improved, but water injection was an emergency only aid, intended for short bursts of power.

From late November 1943 the aircraft strength of the 56th had gradually been increased from 75 to near 100, thus enabling the group to sortie

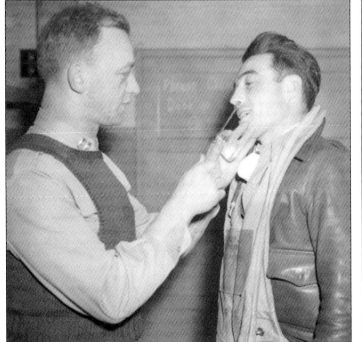

Each squadron had a Flight Surgeon who kept a regular check on the pilot's physical and mental health. Hear, Capt George Horning checks 1Lt Milton Anderson's ears. Anderson, a combat original in the 61st FS, never had an opportunity to attack enemy aircraft during his tour

'Doc' Horning gives Lt Eugene Barnum a nasal spray. Respiratory infections were the biggest cause of pilots being told they must not fly. Barnum was killed in a combat collision during his second tour with the 56th. He claimed two aerial victories during his service in the ETO

43

Col Robert Landry poses in the cockpit of his fighter with a station pet. Landry was the ex-VIII Fighter Command staff officer who commanded the group during 'Hub' Zemke's absence in the autumn of 1943. He destroyed one enemy aircraft, on 11 December 1943, during his brief spell in command. Later, in 1945, Landry was put in charge of the B-17G-equipped 493rd Bomb Group

Coming home over the cold cruel North Sea. P-47C 41-6385/HV-Y was first assigned to Lt Robill Roberts, but in December 1943 Claude Mussey took it over. Following his loss over the North Sea in March 1944, the fighter passed into general use, before being retired to the 495th FTG in May 1944 – by which time it was the last P-47C in service with the 56th FG

62nd FS Engineering Officer, 1Lt Edwin Maxfield, watches work being carried out on *"HAWKEYE"* (P-47D 42-75125/LM-E). This particular Thunderbolt was received by the 56th FG in December 1943, and initially went into general use, before being assigned to Lt Thaddeus Buszko in February 1944. Maxfield was noted for many excellent engineer-ing ideas, although his most publicised 'claim to fame' was filling clean drop tanks with an ice cream mixture and having them flown to 20,000 ft for a Sunday treat!

two separate formations when tasked with providing bomber escort. Two independent groups greatly increased the cover available.

The first of these so-called A and B group missions was undertaken on 11 January 1944, with three 12-aeroplane squadron formations in each group. Only the A group saw action on this day when the bombers came under concentrated attack, claims of ten destroyed, two probables and seven damaged being made for no loss. 1Lt Glen Schiltz was credited with three of these destroyed claims, giving him his second triple on a single mission.

On 19 January 1944 'Hub' Zemke arrived back at Halesworth to reclaim his command. There had been a move to retain him in the Zone of the Interior, as the military establishment in the USA was officially

Several of the group's pilots found themselves short of fuel when they returned from the 3 February 1944 mission. Lt John Fields was one of them, and he got within five miles of Halesworth when the tank of his P-47D 42-7938/LM-<u>S</u> ran dry and he bellied in at Lyons Farm, Bulcamp. This aircraft was originally assigned to Dave Schilling (note his distinctive 'Hairless Joe' motif still worn on the fighter's cowling), who exchanged it for a new improved D-model in January 1944 . . .

termed, but getting wind of this, Zemke quickly removed himself back to the UK by cutting his own orders and hitching a lift on transport aircraft.

While Landry was CO, Maj Francis Gabreski had acted as Deputy Flying Executive to alternate mission leads with Schilling, and Zemke now made this a permanent post – Maj James Stewart replaced 'Gabby' as the 61st FS CO. Gabreski was the leader of B group on 30 January when the 56th had another very successful day. Without incurring any losses, it pilots scored 11 victories, and A group, led by Schilling, three.

The 56th FG endorsed its commanding position among the USAAF fighter groups flying from Britain by claiming its 200th victory on this day, which meant its tally was exactly double that of the second most successful group, the 4th FG. Mahurin raised his score to 15 during this mission, while Robert Johnson ran him close with 14 and Gabreski 11. The pilots who had high scores of victories were mostly squadron and flight leaders, proving once again that opportunity was still a major factor when it came to attaining aerial success.

. . . and this is the aircraft that Schilling was assigned as a replacement for 42-7938 – P-47D 42-75237, which was again coded LM-S. Note the pilot's adoption of the word *WHACK!* and the greatly modified 'Hairless Joe' insignia. The yellow nose band was also a new addition to aircraft assigned to the 62nd FS, which maintained Schilling's P-47s throughout his time with the 56th FG. This view shows the aircraft sat on its hardstanding at Halesworth in February 1944. The fighter has also been fitted with a 'teardrop' perspex panel on either side of the sliding cockpit canopy to give the pilot better rearward vision. The drop tank is a 150-US gallon type

Capt Bob Lamb is seen in the cockpit of his P-47D 42-75053/HV-L on 6 February 1944 – the day after he had shot down a Bf 109 to become an ace. This fifth kill (of seven in total) provided a rather gruesome incident when the German pilot bailed out into Lamb's fire and was mutilated. Individual aircraft letters with a bar underneath were introduced when the complements of squadrons were gradually raised from 25 to 36 fighters apiece, beginning in late November 1943. The aircraft received were new model D-10s and -15s, and many old hands like Lamb took these – he shed his HV-L for HV-<u>L</u>

On 3 February Maj Horace Craig, CO of the 62nd, passed the 200-hour mark in operational flying – the established point at which a fighter pilot was to be rested. He was the first 56th pilot to complete a tour, yet during nine months and some 80 missions, Craig only once had an opportunity to shoot down an enemy aircraft. His replacement as 62nd FS CO was Capt Leroy Schreiber, who had joined the 56th FG soon after it had arrived in the ETO. Once in-theatre, he had quickly impressed Zemke with his team spirit, possibly due to former service as an instructor.

Later in February high command again came proselytising experienced leaders, resulting in 63rd FS CO 'Sy' Burke being posted to the 2nd Bomb Division as a fighter liaison officer. He was replaced in turn by Gerald Johnson, a gifted shot who, with another successful pilot, John Vogt, had been detached to raise the experience level of the 356th FG during the early winter.

THE 'WOLFPACK'

By early 1944, the 56th FG was showing the way to the other American fighter units in England, and promotion of its achievements had the result of creating a competitive spirit among the remaining groups in VIII Fighter Command. Col Zemke was receptive to ideas that he thought would further improve the group's standing, and one of these was the reintroduction of brightly-coloured nose bands for each unit.

All P-47s flying in the UK had hitherto sported white nose bands as a type identity marking, radial-engined fighters tending to be thought of as Fw 190s by those ill versed in aircraft recognition. Luftwaffe *Staffeln* often had the noses of their aircraft painted red or yellow, and it was suggested that if the group's P-47s appeared with similar decor, and the white type identity bands were removed, they might be mistaken by the Luftwaffe for their own kind. With VIII Fighter Command approval, in early February the white nose bands on Halesworth Thunderbolts were replaced with red for the 61st, yellow for the 62nd and light blue for the 63rd FSs – repainting was accomplished in just one night!

Capt Eugene O'Neill was an original combat pilot with the 62nd FS, and he finished his 200-hour tour on 20 February 1944. He was credited with destroying four enemy aircraft in the air and sharing in the destruction of a fifth. Four of these victories were obtained while flying his beloved *Jesse-O* (P-47C 41-6347/LM-O), which also carried the name "*Lil*" *Abner* on the cowling. It was first named *Miss Jesse*, and later had *Torchy* painted below the left side of the cockpit. Nickname changes were common on fighter aircraft, particularly when a new pilot took over. *Jesse-O* was retired to the 495th FTG in January 1944

Lt Fred Christensen of the 62nd FS rated ace after shooting down a Bf 109 on 11 February 1944, and he is seen here posing with his Assistant Crew Chief, Urbain Hymel, alongside his P-47D 42-75207/LM-C. He used this aircraft to claim 10.5 kills between 1 December 1943 and 16 March 1944. Christensen's final wartime tally was an impressive 21.5 aerial victories

There is no evidence to suggest that the Luftwaffe was caught out by this display, but it led to other Eighth Air Force fighter groups requesting to use similar bright markings. The Command resolved the situation by deciding to develop distinctive nose colour markings to represent each of its groups' aircraft, hitherto their having only been squadron identification through fuselage code letters. It was some weeks before this system was brought into effect.

Gen Doolittle, in his capacity as the Eighth's new commander, had early in the new year given permission for his fighters to go down and strafe enemy airfields once their escort duties were over. By this time, with some 1000 fighters available, a relay system had become the main method of support, each fighter group being given a defined area through which to shepherd the bombers until they were relieved by another group.

The first ground strafing by the 56th occurred on 11 February, when after engaging in air-to-air combat they returned to find the B-17s they had previously been escorting guarded by other fighters. Col Zemke then spotted an airfield near Reims – later identified as Juvincourt – and led his force down to shoot up parked aircraft. A Bf 109 that caught the full force of Zemke's guns was the first of many enemy aircraft destroyed by the 56th on the ground.

A period of good weather in late February 1944 enabled the USAAF to press home attacks against the German aircraft industry. Strong opposition was anticipated, and realised. P-51 Mustangs, then still only opera-

The concentrated fire from a P-47's eight 'point fifties' puts paid to a rocket-carrying Bf 110

tional in limited numbers, provided support to the most distant targets, leaving the most experienced P-47 groups to be employed to the limit of their endurance.

On 20 Febraury the 56th reaped the benefit of 150-US gallon tanks for the first time, these stores allowing the Thunderbolts to be airborne for three hours. The group flew to Dümmer Lake, located north of Osnabruck, which would become a familiar point of reference for the 56th on many missions. North-east of Minden, Lt Col Gabreski took the 61st FS down to attack a formation of Bf 110s estimated to be six miles to one side of the bomber stream, and some 7000 ft lower.

As on previous occasions the twin-engined fighters were decimated, 11 being shot down and a dozen damaged. 1Lt Robert Johnson claimed two which made him the leading Eighth Air Force fighter ace with 16. Captain Leroy Schreiber, leading the 62nd Fighter Squadron formation in B group, went after some Me 109s that were attacking the bombers and shot down three. Again the 56th suffered no losses. The advantage the American pilots had was that the Luftwaffe fighters main objective was interception of the B-17s and B-24s and while concentrating on this commitment they were frequently vulnerable to surprise attacks from the bombers' escorts.

Now an efficient fighting team with good air discipline and aggressive leadership, the 56th was in the forefront of the American fighter counter-offensive. The attitude that pervaded pilot get-togethers at Halesworth was that of the hunter, for the Luftwaffe opponents came increasingly to be considered prey. The group had even dubbed itself the Wolfpack which the press would quickly embrace as Zemke's Wolfpack.

On 21 February the group's involvement in combat brought claims of 12 enemy destroyed. One of these fell to Squadron Leader Michael Gladych, one of two officers from RAF Polish manned squadrons who were flying with the 56th. Both had been put on rest status from operational flying but were not happy about this so had approached Gabreski to volunteer to fly with the USAAF.

Zemke was pleased to take experienced pilots and four other Poles were attracted to come to the 56th during the spring of 1944. Zemke also wel-

comed several bomber pilots who having finished their tours in B-17s or B-24s wanted to transfer to fighters. A total of 17 victories were claimed for the air fighting next day once more without loss. No wonder the area around Dümmer Lake became know as the 'Happy Hunting Ground,' among 56th pilots. This day the 61st became the first fighter squadron in the Eighth to be credited with 100 enemy aircraft shot down.

Action on the 24th brought nine more victories, but the group also suffered its first loss for a dozen missions – and this pilot, Lt Wilbur Kelley, was a victim of ground fire when his flight went down to strafe an enemy airfield. The Luftwaffe was less in evidence for the group during the last three missions of February, by which time VIII Fighter Command was able to put near 700 fighters into the air, and RAF Fighter Command gave support in coastal regions of the continent. The Luftwaffe fighter force was being effectively overwhelmed.

Early in March 1944 the Eighth Air Force turned its attention to targets in the enemy capital. Strong Luftwaffe opposition was expected, and weather frustrated the first attempts, with only a few B-17s bombing Berlin on the 4th. Two days later the Eighth was able to attack in force,

These two photographs were taken during the afternoon sleet and snow showers that swept over Halesworth on 22 February 1944. All three aircraft are yellow-nosed P-47s from the 'Wolfpack's' 62nd FS. Both LM-E, flown by Lt Buszko, and Lt Carcione's LM-Q picked up flak splinters in the left wing and tail respectively during a mission flown earlier that day. The cowling motif of Carcione's *Sex Wagon* still exists as an exhibit in the Norfolk and Suffolk Aviation Museum at Flixton

A highly-polished *SNEAKY M^cGEE* sits unattended on its Halesworth hardstanding soon after being received by the 62nd FS in mid-February 1944. The new LM-<u>S</u> was first assigned to Lt Wendell McClure, and by coincidence, there was also a Jim McClure flying with the squadron at this time, and one of the first 62nd pilots lost in the ETO was John McClure. The aircraft retains the standard white noseband, possibly because group colour markings were in the offing. The group painted out the white type identity bands on empenages when coloured noses were introduced, the 56th believing these to be of greater advantage to enemy pilots than to friendly

Lt William Janson flew a complete tour with the 56th FG, but like many other wingmen, he never had an opportunity to shoot down an enemy aircraft. He inherited P-47D 42-8410/UN-U from 1Lt John Coenen, who was the 63rd FS's Operations Officer. Crew chief S/Sgt Dan Burch leans on the fighter's cowling, while his assistant, Sgt John Murphy, stands on the wing. *Betty Ann II* was eventually retired from the frontline and passed to the ASR squadron, then based at Boxted

Bob Johnson's assigned aircraft was used for this photographic pose by Capt Walker 'Bud' Mahurin after he had been credited with 15 aerial victories on 3 February 1944

and the anticipated Luftwaffe reaction materialised. The air battles of 6 March resulted in 69 'heavies' and 11 fighters failing to return, which would prove to be the heaviest combat loss sustained by the USAAF during its operations from the UK. In return, the Luftwaffe suffered the loss of some 70 fighters, of which the 56th claimed ten.

Two days later the bombers made for Berlin again, and in this 'Happy Hunting Ground' the 56th ran up record claims of 27 destroyed and two probables, taking the group's credits to a record 300 enemy aircraft destroyed. But from the fighting on 8 March five pilots failed to return, with one known to have gone down to flak and the other four falling as a result of aerial combat.

'Bud' Mahurin was credited with triple victories after this mission, boosting his total to 20, and allowing him to assume the position of leading ETO ace from the 353rd FG's Walter Beckham, who had overtaken the 56th FG pilot just two days earlier. A week later 'Bob' Johnson claimed three enemy fighters out of 24 credited to the 56th, exceeding Mahurin's tally in the process. Next day another Ramrod yielded 11 victories over single-engined fighters without a single loss being incurred. For its achievements during the period 20 February to 9 March 1944, the 56th

On bleak 14 March 1944 the 'Top Brass' paid a visit to Halesworth. Seen hear discussing drop tanks are, from left to right, Maj Gen James Doolittle, Brig Gen Jesse Auton (CG of the 65th FW), Lt Col David Schilling, Lt Gen Carl Spaatz and Col Zemke

was awarded a Distinguished Unit Citation (DUC), which is the highest award of distinction for United States' military organisations.

In mid-March the nose bands of all 56th Thunderbolts were painted red as a group identity marking, whilst other VIII Fighter Command groups were assigned colours, or combinations thereof in checkerboard. The 56th still strove to be distinctive, however, and moved the squadron colours to the aircraft rudders, with the exception of the 63rd FS, who kept their tails painted olive drab.

Groups equipped with the long-range P-51B Mustangs were now increasingly those who made the highest claims of Luftwaffe fighters. In an effort to increase the chance of contact, the 56th despatched three separate forces at different times on a single operation on 22 March, the A group consisting of 36 P-47s, the B group 25 and C group just 8.

It proved to be a disappointing day, for there was no air combat and B group lost four aircraft. One was shot down while strafing in Holland, with the pilot surviving, and three others disappeared climbing into an overcast above the North Sea. Nothing more was heard, but collisions were suspected. The mission of 27 March also did nothing for group morale, the bombers being sent to various targets in France and the 56th being given the task of providing withdrawal support. Four P-47s failed to return, two of which were flown by leading aces Walker Mahurin and Gerald Johnson.

Johnson's aircraft was hit by small arms fire while strafing, forcing him to hastily crash-land in a field. Mahurin bailed out after his P-47's engine was hit by return fire from a Do 217 bomber that he had attacked south of Chartres. Another P-47 was also seen to 'belly in' as a result of ground fire, while the fourth Thunderbolt lost suffered similar damage, causing its pilot to bail out over the sea, where he drowned. Johnson was made a PoW, but Mahurin managed to evade capture, eventually returning to the UK in early May.

To add to the gloom, on the 29th two B-24s collided and crashed close to Halesworth, and in trying to rescue the crews six USAAF men from Halesworth were killed and 33 wounded when part of a bomb load exploded. One helper losing his life was 1Lt Stanley 'Fats' Morrill, who had shot down his ninth enemy aircraft on 16 March.

COMBAT REPORT

On 27 March the 56th lost two of its most distinguished pilots, Walker Mahurin and Gerald Johnson. Mahurin evaded capture and later returned to the UK, but Johnson was taken prisoner. Maj Gerald Johnson's flight consisted of Lt Everett, the major's wingman, and Lt Robey leading the second element, with Lt Lovett as his wingman. The following is 1Lt Archie Robey's account of what happened;

'After we had dropped down to find an airport or some other target to strafe, I fired at some high tension wires in the vicinity of Lassay, and saw one pole and wires fall to the ground. At approximately 1545 hours we sighted some trucks with soldiers in them, and Maj Johnson, Lt Everett and myself went down to attack (Lt Lovett had had supercharger trouble when we were with the bombers and had to drop down. We did not hear from him so he never could join up with us). We then strafed and severely damaged some of the trucks.

'After we had made a couple of passes on different trucks, we headed out to the coast. At that time someone called in a line of trucks to our right, just entering a small town. We then flew over the town of Conde to see if we could sight them. As we passed over Conde at about a thousand feet, my plane was hit by .303 and 20 mm fire. I caught up with Maj Johnson, and after we had gone approximately five miles east, he called to say he was hit and was crash-landing

'Lt Everett and myself circled and saw him belly in an open field. Maj Johnson then got out of his plane and then apparently opened his parachute in the cockpit and set it on fire, as smoke was coming from the cockpit. I called Yardstick and said "Postgate White 1 has landed on his belly. I think I can land. Shall I go down and pick him up?" To this Yardstick (Lt Col Schilling) answered "Roger, Roger". I then lowered my wheels, but my flaps would not come down due to the battle damage my plane had received. Not being able to cut my speed I was unable to land in such a small field. However, as I was circling round I saw Maj Johnson surrounded by a group of civilians, all of whom were shaking his hand, and with his free hand he waved me on. He then started to run towards the adjoining woods, accompanied by the civilians.

'Lt Everett and I then headed for the coast on the deck, but I was forced to go rather slowly as I could only get me wheels half way up. As we approached landfall out at Arromanches, I was again hit by .303 and 20 mm guns, and I believe Lt Everett's plane was also hit at this time. Once we were out of range we climbed to 2000 ft. About five miles off the coast I saw Lt Everett turn around and head back towards the French coast. As he had not said anything over the R/T, I switched to "B" Channel on which I then heard him give a Mayday. I then called him and he then told me he was going to ditch the plane. I told him not to ditch but to bail out. There was nothing further that I could do for him as I was unable to go back with him due to my latest battle damage.

'I then called Tackline (65th FW control) and gave them a Mayday for Lt Everett. Tackline answered that they were sending out an Air-Sea Rescue launch for him. For the next ten minutes I kept calling Tackline to relay Lt Everett's position in relation to mine. From the R/T I gathered a plane was about a mile or so from where Lt Everett's plane would have gone down.

'On arriving at Ford, an RAF base on the south coast of England, I had considerable difficulty in landing. My wheels were still down. My flaps would not work. My prop was in fixed pitch and my right tyre was shot up. I was forced to go around quite a few times as I could not cut my speed, and furthermore, Mustangs were continually blocking the runways. As I landed my engine completely froze and I was forced to skid off the runway to come to a dead stop.'

By the time the ASR launch reached the spot where Everett's P-47 went down there was no sign of the pilot. The cold Channel had claimed another victim. A few weeks later the cruel sea also took Archie Robey's life.

The early missions of April 1944 were nowhere near as fruitful as those flown just a month before. The Luftwaffe was still being dominated by VIII Fighter Command, but most of the action, and success, centred around the longer-ranged Mustangs.

Nevertheless, Bob Johnson raised his leading score to 23 air victories on the 9th and 25 on the 11th. Strafing now became a regular business if fuel and ammunition remained, and on the 15th the number of aircraft destroyed on the ground was for the first time higher than those shot out of the sky – 12 as against 5. In fact, on this day the group, along with others, took part in the first JACKPOT operation, which was a planned strafing of enemy airfield targets in designated areas. The weather was bad, causing several groups to abandone their missions, but the 56th endured.

At Husum/Flensburg airfield Zemke led the 61st FS down to shoot up He 111s parked in revetments. Eight were credited as destroyed and several probably, or damaged. Zemke demolished three of these, and his gun camera film of this action became the most frequently seen sequence of aircraft being strafed in post-war documentaries. If the full dangers of ground attack had not hitherto been appreciated they were this day.

Two of the 56th's veteran pilots went down to ground fire, namely 12-kill ace Maj Leroy Schreiber (the 62nd's CO) and Capt Richard Mudge of the 61st. Mudge lived, but the talented Schreiber was killed. A third loss that day was fellow veteran Capt Charles Harrison, who fell to the guns of an Fw 190. The attrition through ground attack led VIII Fighter Command to issue a statement that aircraft destroyed on the ground rated equal to those shot out of the sky in assessing pilots' achievements. Thereafter press releases gave equal prominence to air and ground credits.

Zemke moved Maj Lucian Dade from Group Operations to take over the 62nd. A few days earlier he had returned Gabreski to the 61st as CO in the wake of Maj James Stewart being ordered to VIII Fighter Com-

A He 111 explodes in flame, this aircraft being one of three Heinkel bombers 'Hub' Zemke destroyed during a strafing attack on the dispersal area at Husum on 15 April 1944

Maj Leroy Schreiber, CO of the 62nd FS, was one of the most popular and promising pilots in the 56th, claiming 12 aerial victories, 1 probable, 6 damaged and 2 destroyed on the ground between 30 July 1943 and 9 April 1944. He lost his life on 15 April 1944 when his P-47D 43-25577/LM-T was shot down by ground fire while strafing Flensburg airfield

mand HQ. In the days immediately prior to these command changes, the 56th had been notified that it would have to move to an airfield called Boxted on the outskirts of the town of Colchester, some 40 miles south of Halesworth. There was little enthusiasm for the move, although the group was pleased to find that the facilities were complete, and mud did not predominate.

Like Halesworth, which was wanted for a new B-24 group on its way over from the US, Boxted had been built to a similar specification as a bomber base. The creation of the Fifteenth Air Force in Italy late the previous year, and the diversion of many bomber groups originally destined for the Eighth, had led to a surplus of bomber airfields in East Anglia which then became available for fighter use.

The main move to Boxted took place on 18 April, when both A and B groups, despatched on an uneventful mission from Halesworth, landed at Boxted. For Dave Schilling it was his last lead before 30 days rest and recuperation in the USA. This was an alternative offered to pilots who wished to return to operations with their current unit, rather than be reassigned following the completion of their 200 combat hours tour. Both 50-hour and 25-hour extensions were permitted if requested, but in late April a tour was extended to 300 hours when the number of tour completions threatened to be greater than the supply of replacement pilots. Hal Comstock, Donovan Smith, Joe Egan and George Hall were other original combat pilots who also left for home following the move to Boxted.

BOXTED AND D-DAY

T he first 15 missions flown from Boxted yielded only one aerial victory in the shape of an unfortunate Ju 88 caught in transit near Paris. Frustrated in the air, the 56th turned its attention to enemy airfields, and on the 24th had a particularly successful outing. At Thalheim 14 aircraft were credited as destroyed, whilst a further 15 at this and other Luftwaffe bases suffered some degree of damage.

On the 27th a group formation went out under Type 16 control. This was the code name for an RAF ground radar directed system where any hostile tracks in range were reported to the fighter leader, who could then manoeuvre for attack. The sweep over Pas de Calais and the Low Countries was uneventful, and although these radar-controlled missions became a frequent task, they rarely proved fruitful, for by this date the Luftwaffe had well and truly lost control of the skies over this area of occupied Europe.

During another Type 16 sweep flown the very next day, several enemy fighters were observed on Orleans/Bricy airfield. An attack mission was quickly organised at Boxted, with 'Hub' Zemke in the lead. Once reports of the enemy fighters had been been received by the 56th FG, Zemke

On 8 May 1944 an exploding shell riddled Lt Thaddeus Buszko's P-47D 42-75125/LM-E with splinters in its wings, fuselage and tail, as well as causing an engine fire which the pilot extinguished by going into a dive. Back at Boxted, *Hawkeye* was a sorry sight

obtained permission to conduct a dive-bombing raid on the German airfield – he had his armourers hastily install M41 fragmentation bomb clusters on 24 P-47s. Frustratingly, by the time the 56th arrived over the target, cloud cover in the Orleans area had increased to a point where it was not possible to see the airfield. The bombs were eventually dropped on another unidentified airfield north of Paris during a series of diving attacks that saw the P-47s descend for around 3000 ft, before the pilots launched their ordnance at altitudes between 11,000 and 13,000 ft. Some of the bombs hung up and had to be brought back to base – a highly undesirable situation – but all aircraft landed safely.

At the beginning of May the 56th received notice that a provisional air-sea rescue squadron was to be formed at Boxted, and that the group would assist in this formation. War-weary P-47s equipped the unit, these being fitted out with flare rack and dinghy-pack installations. Pilots were selected from all VIII Fighter Command groups, or from those taken off combat operations for one reason or another. Located at the northern end of the airfield, the 'ASR Squadron', as it was usually known, stayed at Boxted until January 1945, when it moved to Halesworth to expand. Many of the unit's original aircraft were well-worn P-47Ds from the 56th.

Capt Robert S Johnson, who had been transferred from the 61st to the 62nd FS early in May to serve as a flight leader, shot down a Bf 109 and a Fw 190 on 8 May to reinforce his position as the USAAF's top ace in Europe. These kills took his total to 27 aerial victories, a tally higher than

Capt Robert Johnson is seen on 8 May 1944 in a congratulatory pose with S/Sgt J C Penrod, the crew chief of *Penrod & Sam* (P-47D 42-25512/LM-Q) in which Bob's 26th and 27th victories had been made earlier that day. Soon after the 56th FG arrived at Boxted, Bob Johnson was transferred from the 61st to the 62nd FS, where he became a flight commander

A mechanic takes a break on the tailplane of 'Hub' Zemke's P-47D 42-76471/UN-Z, the aircraft being parked on its usual hardstanding at Boxted. Just to the left of the rudder can be seen the two small hangars where Redwing biplanes were built in the early 1930s

An enemy fighter hit by Zemke's fire goes down on 12 May 1944; 'This Me 109 was caught assembling with a formation at 28,000 ft between Frankfurt and Wiesbaden. He just turned into a climbing left turn. With a couple of rings lead at 250 to 300 yards, he was allowed to fly thru five seconds of fire from eight machine guns'. This kill made Zemke a double ace

the combined air and ground credits of the 4th FG's Don Gentile, who had hitherto been publicised as the Eighth's leading ace.

In later years Bob Johnson's score was elevated to 28 through reassessment of his gun camera film, and later still returned to 27. In most cases, the precise number of enemy aircraft shot down by a pilot is subject to doubt, with some destroyed credits being given for aircraft which are now known to have survived, while others categorised as damaged actually fell.

On the same day that Johnson claimed his final two victories whilst participating in a group-strength escort mission in support of bombers going to Berlin and Brunswick, yet another example of bad aircraft recognition almost resulted in fratricide.

The group's only loss on 8 May was 2Lt Gordon Lewis, a 62nd FS wingman who was shot down by a 352nd FG P-51 during a mêlée in the 'Happy Hunting Ground'. Lewis was able to take to his parachute. What exasperated the 56th leadership was that while they only had a total of six air credits for the day, the 352nd's Mustangs had 27 – the largest proportion of the 44 claimed by Mustangs. Thunderbolt units, on the other hand, could muster only nine claims for the day, and the Lightning groups just six. The Mustang's ascendancy was now abundantly clear.

Frustrated, the aggressive Zemke looked for ways to better the 56th's chances of engaging the enemy, and he duly came up with the tactic that became known as the 'Zemke Fan'. The plan called for a P-47 formation to fly to a good visual reference point in enemy territory such as a lake or a river, and then for the four-aeroplane flights to separate and fan out in different directions, with a close concentration in the centre to be called in if contact was made with the enemy.

The 'Zemke Fan' was first tried on 12 May – the date the Eighth Air Force commenced its campaign against German synthetic oil production, which was rigorously opposed by the Luftwaffe. Zemke set off from Boxted with a 24-strong A group to sweep ahead of the bombers in the Frankfurt area. A distinctive curve in the Rhine, some 36 miles south of

Lt Robert Rankin splays his fingers to represent the five Bf 109s that he shot down on 12 May 1944 flying 42-25836/HV-M

Capt Joe Powers and his wingman, Flt Off Joe Vitale, were credited with bringing down a Bf 109 that is believed to have been flown by Günther Rall, the Luftwaffe's third-ranking ace with 276 victories. This kill was claimed on 12 May, bringing Powers' final tally to 14.5 aerial victories and five damaged. Tour-expired, he transferred out of the 56th FG just days later. Powers was subsequently killed in action flying a F-51D Mustang with the 67th FBS/18th FBG in Korea on 18 January 1951

S/Sgt Damon Itza poses with a pet kid beside Col Zemke's P-47D 42-26413/UN-Z – the first 'bubble top' Thunderbolt received by the 56th. This was a presentation aircraft, with the acknowledgement *OREGONIS BRITANNIA* being painted on the fuselage just forward of the D-Day stripes

Tail wheels off, P-47D 42-25517/LM-X
***Miss Take* and P-47D 42-26636/LM-X**
of the 62nd FS gather speed on
Boxted runway One Zero in late June
1944. **This was the view from the**
base control tower

Coblenz, was the point where the formation dispersed, each of the six flights spreading out so as to form a 180-degree 'fan' over the Coblenz-Giessen-Frankfurt area.

A shallow climb had been made to this point in order to conserve fuel and prolong duration. Zemke's flight in the centre was at 20,000 ft when it was suddenly bounced from above by a *Staffel* of Bf 109s. One of the flight wingmen had earlier turned back with mechanical trouble, and the remaining three P-47s were left in a perilous position. Zemke took them into a defensive circle but to no avail, for two of the Thunderbolts were swiftly shot down by the leading Bf 109 pilot, who made diving attacks and then recovered altitude to repeat the procedure.

Aware that he was next in line, Zemke put his P-47 into a violent decent and was not pursued. Regaining altitude, he came across a large assembly of enemy fighters and called for help, which was eventually answered by 1Lts Robert Rankin and Cleon Thomton – the latter on his first combat mission. 'Shorty' Rankin and his wingman had already been involved in a series of successful air combats prior to joining up with the colonel who, after picking off one of the Messerschmits, had to turn for home due to a diminishing fuel supply.

The day's fighting produced 18 destroyed credits – taking the 56th's total past the 400 mark – for the loss of three P-47s, whose pilots, it was

Gathered in front of the redoubtable *Silver Lady*, five of the 'Polish Flight', established within the 61st FS, pose with Gabreski who, on detachment, had flown Spitfires with RAF-controlled Polish unit No 315 Sqn. They are, left to right, Boleslaw Gladych, Tadeusz Sawicz, 'Gabby' Gabreski, Kazimierz Rutkowski, Tadeusz Andersz and Witold Lanowski. An additional Polish pilot, Zbigniew Janicki, was killed a week after D-Day when his P-47 crashed near Le Mans after reportedly being struck by flak. On 'secondment' from the RAF, the remaining Poles – bar Gladych and Lanowski – eventually returned to their former service. Both 'Mike' Gladych and 'Lanny' Lanowski stuck with Thunderbolts, flying with the 56th FG until after VE-Day

later learned, were prisoners. One of those in the Zemke flight was Lt Col Preston Piper, a former bomber pilot who had requested to transfer to fighters after a traumatic experience ditching a B-17. The most successful pilot on this day was 'Shorty' Rankin of the 61st FS, who earned fame by being credited with shooting down five Bf 109s. The first P-47 pilot in the ETO to achieve this feat in a single sortie, Rankin had gone into the mission needing just a solitary kill to 'make ace'.

Another notable action on 12 May – although it was unknown at the time – was that the Bf 109 brought down by Capt Joe Powers (the last of his 14.5 aerial kills) and his wingman, Flt Off Joe Vitale, was that of the great ace Major Gunther Rall, who escaped with severe injuries. Also unknown at the time, Rall, with more than 200 victories to his name, was the pilot who had shot down Zemke's wingmen earlier in the day.

The 'Zemke Fan' had certainly brought contacts with the enemy, but it was clear that dispersing flights over a wide area dissipated strength if the Luftwaffe was encountered in numbers. Its originator identified this weakness first-hand, having twice found himself alone among several enemy fighters, and he was far from keen to repeat the experience.

Next day a support mission by A and B groups for the bombers brought five more aerial victories, following which poor (*text continues on page 81*)

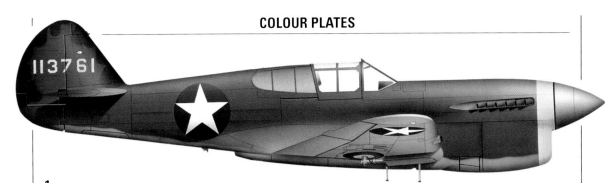

1
P-40F 41-13761 of Lt Eugene O'Neill, 62nd FS, Bendix Airport, New Jersey, April 1942

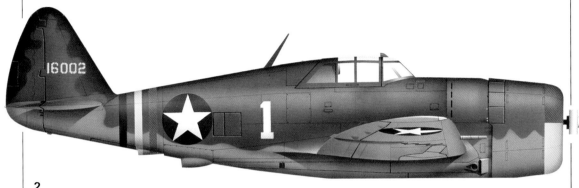

2
P-47B 41-6002 of Col Hubert Zemke, CO of the 56th FG, Bridgeport Municipal Airport, Connecticut, September 1942

3
P-47B 41-5999 of the 61st FS, Bridgeport Municipal Airport, Connecticut, September 1942

4
P-47C-5 41-6352 of Capt Donald Renwick, 61st FS, King's Cliffe, March 1943

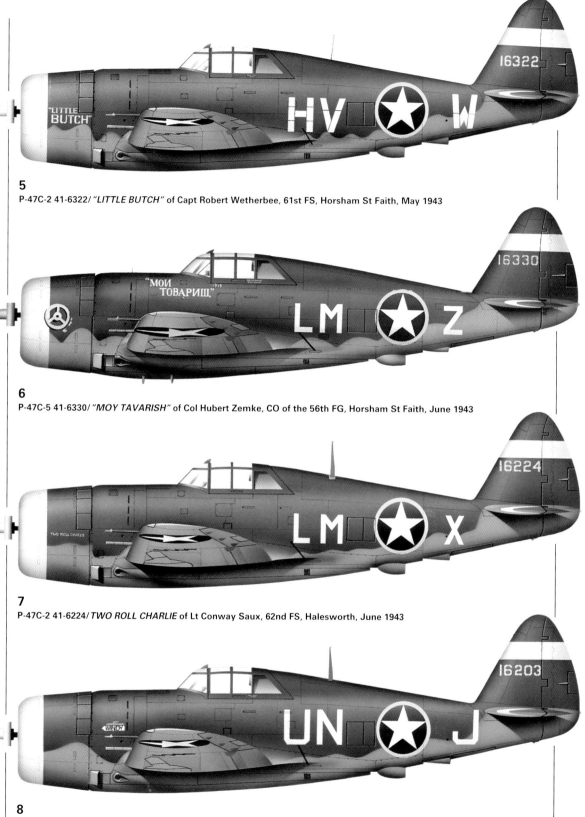

5
P-47C-2 41-6322/ *"LITTLE BUTCH"* of Capt Robert Wetherbee, 61st FS, Horsham St Faith, May 1943

6
P-47C-5 41-6330/ *"MOY TAVARISH"* of Col Hubert Zemke, CO of the 56th FG, Horsham St Faith, June 1943

7
P-47C-2 41-6224/ *TWO ROLL CHARLIE* of Lt Conway Saux, 62nd FS, Halesworth, June 1943

8
P-47C-2 41-6203/ *WINDY* of Lt Jack Brown, 63rd FS, Halesworth, June 1943

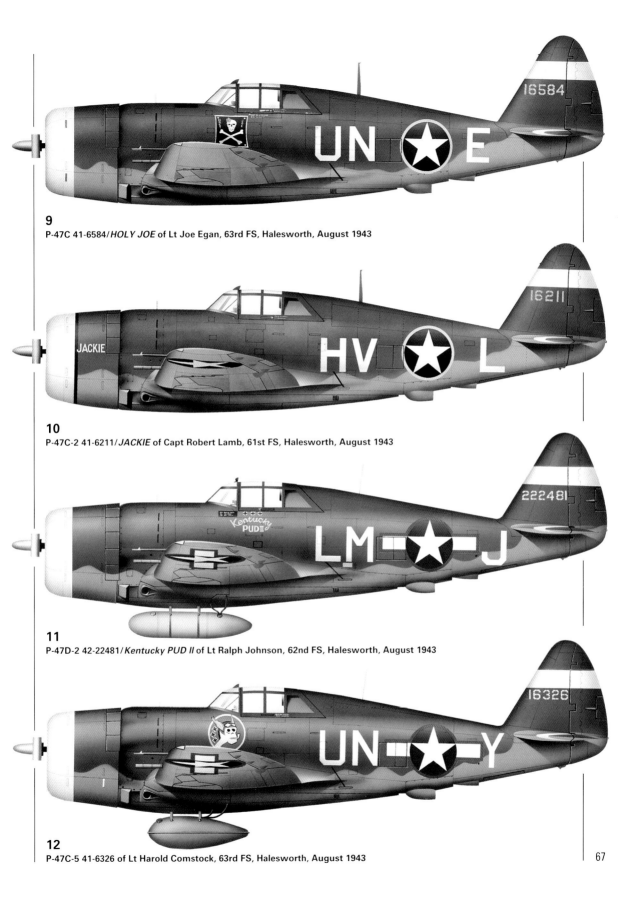

9
P-47C 41-6584/*HOLY JOE* of Lt Joe Egan, 63rd FS, Halesworth, August 1943

10
P-47C-2 41-6211/*JACKIE* of Capt Robert Lamb, 61st FS, Halesworth, August 1943

11
P-47D-2 42-22481/*Kentucky PUD II* of Lt Ralph Johnson, 62nd FS, Halesworth, August 1943

12
P-47C-5 41-6326 of Lt Harold Comstock, 63rd FS, Halesworth, August 1943

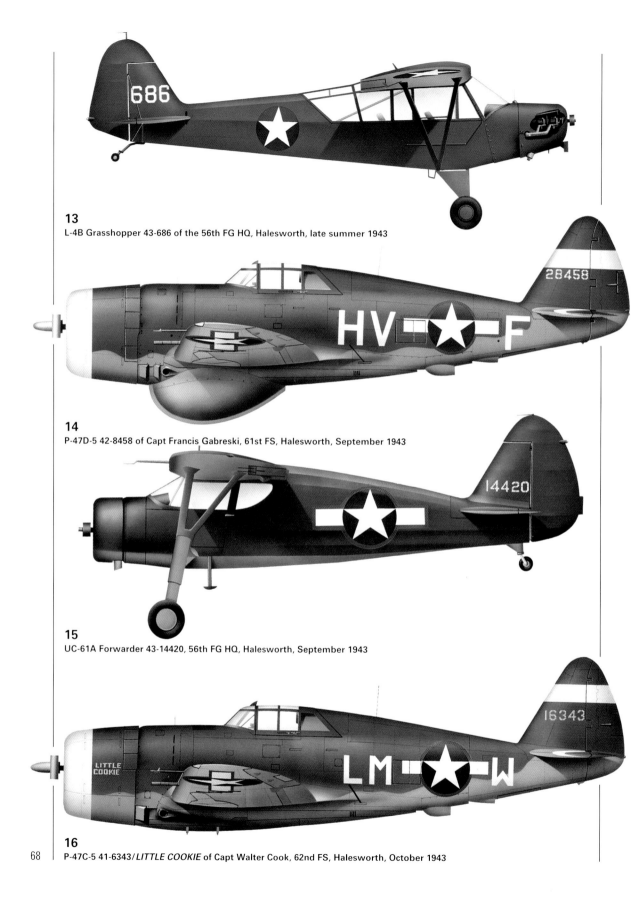

13
L-4B Grasshopper 43-686 of the 56th FG HQ, Halesworth, late summer 1943

14
P-47D-5 42-8458 of Capt Francis Gabreski, 61st FS, Halesworth, September 1943

15
UC-61A Forwarder 43-14420, 56th FG HQ, Halesworth, September 1943

16
P-47C-5 41-6343/*LITTLE COOKIE* of Capt Walter Cook, 62nd FS, Halesworth, October 1943

17
P-47D-1 42-7938/ *"HEWLETT-WOODMERE LONG ISLAND"* of Maj David Schilling, Deputy CO of the 56th FG,
Halesworth, October 1943

18
P-47C-2 41-6259 of Lt Glen Schiltz, 63rd FS, Halesworth, October 1943

19
P-47D-1 42-7877/ *"JACKSON COUNTY. MICHIGAN. FIGHTER"/IN THE MOOD* of Capt Gerald Johnson, 61st FS,
Halesworth, October 1943

20
P-47C-5 41-6325/*'Lucky Little Devil'* of Lt John Vogt, 63rd FS, Halesworth, October 1943

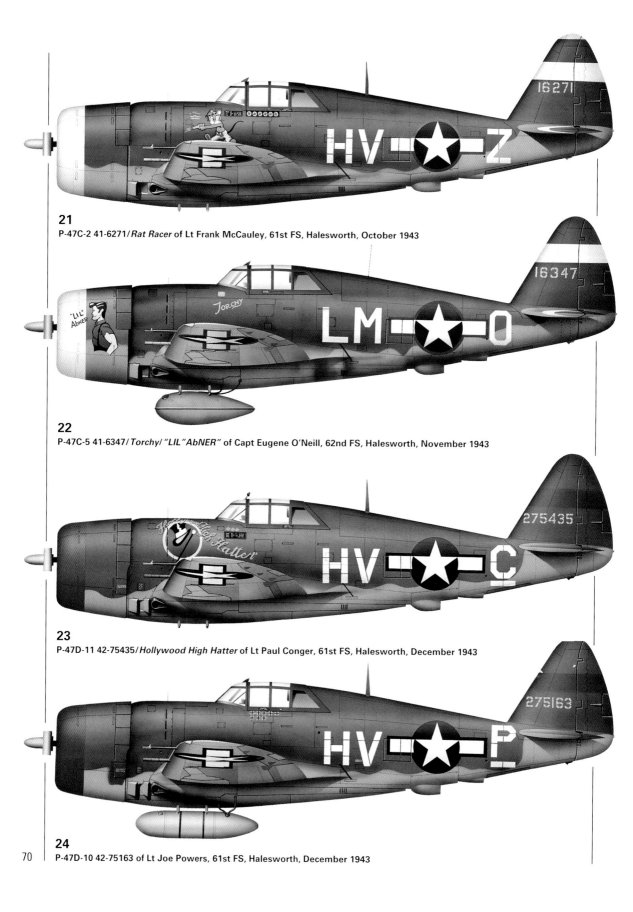

21
P-47C-2 41-6271/*Rat Racer* of Lt Frank McCauley, 61st FS, Halesworth, October 1943

22
P-47C-5 41-6347/*Torchy*/ *"LIL"AbNER"* of Capt Eugene O'Neill, 62nd FS, Halesworth, November 1943

23
P-47D-11 42-75435/*Hollywood High Hatter* of Lt Paul Conger, 61st FS, Halesworth, December 1943

24
P-47D-10 42-75163 of Lt Joe Powers, 61st FS, Halesworth, December 1943

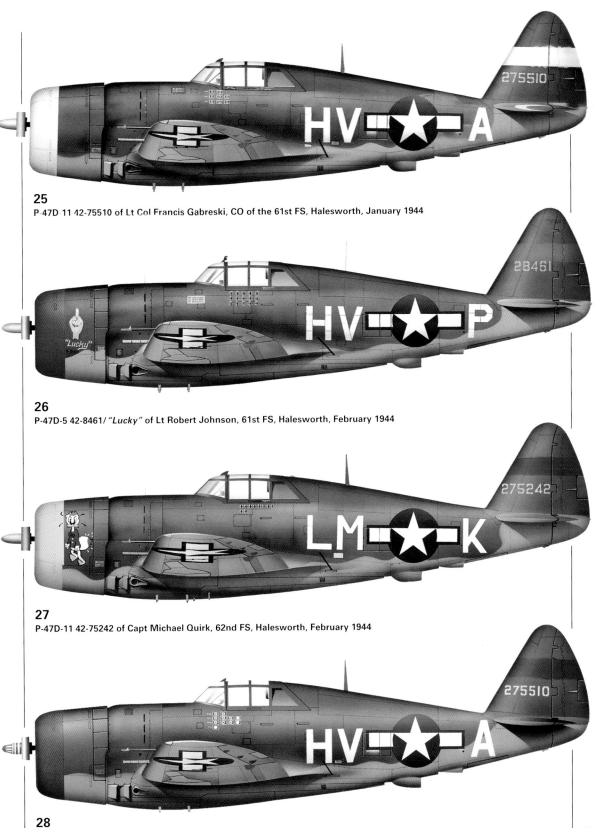

25
P-47D-11 42-75510 of Lt Col Francis Gabreski, CO of the 61st FS, Halesworth, January 1944

26
P-47D-5 42-8461/*"Lucky"* of Lt Robert Johnson, 61st FS, Halesworth, February 1944

27
P-47D-11 42-75242 of Capt Michael Quirk, 62nd FS, Halesworth, February 1944

28
P-47D-11 42-75510 of Lt Col Francis Gabreski, 61st FS, Halesworth, February 1944

29
P-47D-11 42-75237/*WHACK!!* of Lt Col Dave Schilling, Deputy CO of the 56th FG, Halesworth, February 1944

30
P-47D-15 42-75864 of Col Hubert Zemke, CO of the 56th FG, Halesworth, March 1944

31
P-47D-15 42-76179/*Little Chief* of Lt Frank Klibbe, 61st FS, Halesworth, March 1944

32
P-47D-5 42-8487/*"SPIRIT OF ATLANTIC CITY, N.J."* of Capt Walker Mahurin, 63rd FS, Halesworth, March 1944

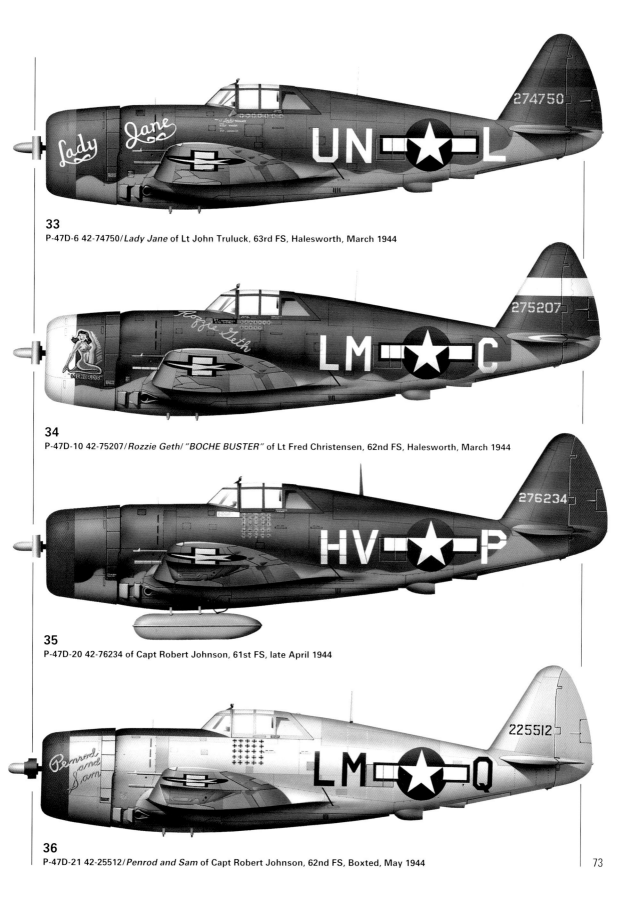

33
P-47D-6 42-74750/*Lady Jane* of Lt John Truluck, 63rd FS, Halesworth, March 1944

34
P-47D-10 42-75207/*Rozzie Geth*/ *"BOCHE BUSTER"* of Lt Fred Christensen, 62nd FS, Halesworth, March 1944

35
P-47D-20 42-76234 of Capt Robert Johnson, 61st FS, late April 1944

36
P-47D-21 42-25512/*Penrod and Sam* of Capt Robert Johnson, 62nd FS, Boxted, May 1944

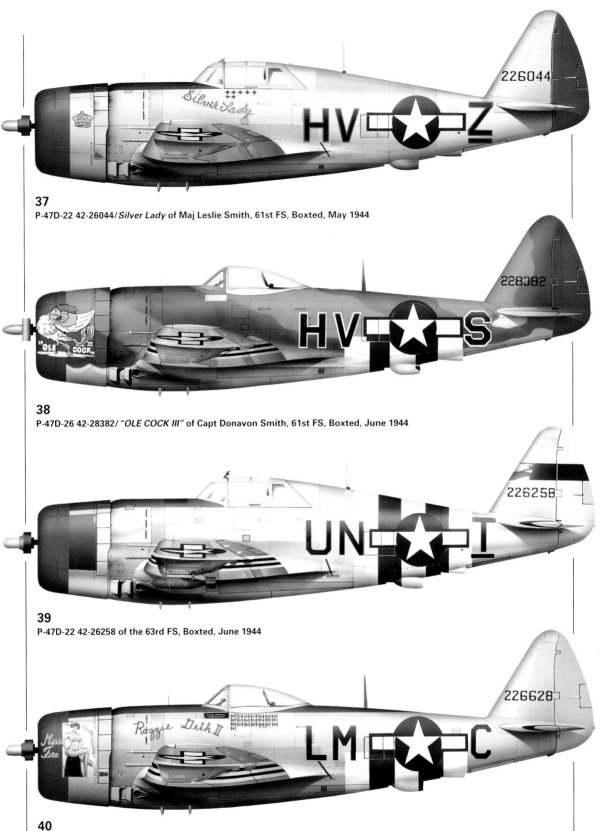

37
P-47D-22 42-26044/*Silver Lady* of Maj Leslie Smith, 61st FS, Boxted, May 1944

38
P-47D-26 42-28382/*"OLE COCK III"* of Capt Donavon Smith, 61st FS, Boxted, June 1944

39
P-47D-22 42-26258 of the 63rd FS, Boxted, June 1944

40
P-47D-25 42-26628/*Rozzie Geth II*/*Miss Fire* of Capt Frederick Christensen, 62nd FS, Boxted, July 1944

41
P-47D-22 42-26298/*Stalag Luft III/I Wanted Wings* of Lt Albert Knafelz, 62nd FS, Boxted, July 1944

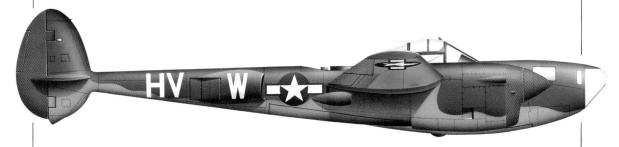

42
P-38J Lightning 'Droop Snoot' of the 61st FS, Boxted, July 1944

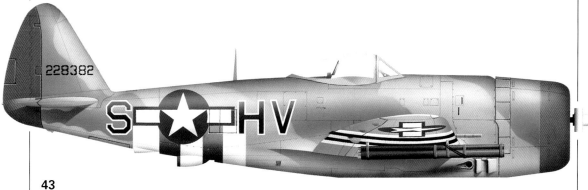

43
P-47D-26 42-28382/*"OLE COCK III"* of Capt Donavon Smith, 61st FS, Boxted, August 1944

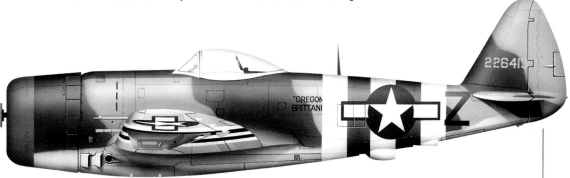

44
P-47D-25 42-26413/*"OREGONS BRITANNIA"* of Col Hubert Zemke, CO of the 56th FG, Boxted, August 1944

45
P-47D-25 42-26413/*"OREGONS BRITANNIA"*/*HAPPY WARRIOR* of Maj Harold E Comstock, CO of the 63rd FS, Boxted, September 1944

46
P-47D-25 42-26466/*ANAMOSA III* of Capt Russell Westfall, 63rd FS, Boxted, September 1944

47
P-47D-11 42-75276/*CATEGORY "E"* of the 63rd FS, Boxted, September 1944

48
P-47M-1 44-21108 of Capt Witold Lanowski, 61st FS, Boxted, March 1945

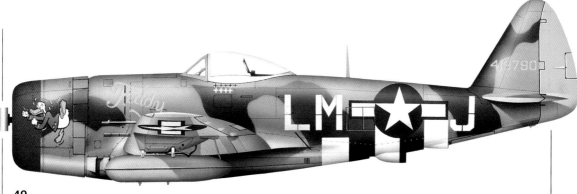

49
P-47D-28 44-19780/*Teddy* of Capt Michael Jackson, 62nd FS, Boxted, November 1944

50
P-47D-22 42-26299 of Capt Cameron Hart, 63rd FS, Boxted, September 1944

51
P-47D-25 42-26641 of Col David Schilling, CO of the 56th FG, Boxted, December 1944

52
P-47M-1 44-21117/*Teddy* of Maj Michael Jackson, 62nd FS, Boxted, February 1945

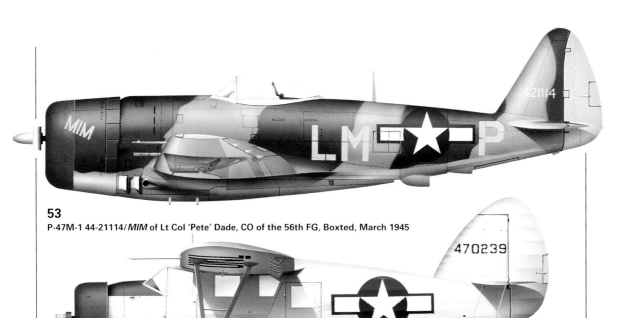

53
P-47M-1 44-21114/*MIM* of Lt Col 'Pete' Dade, CO of the 56th FG, Boxted, March 1945

54
UC-64A Norseman 44-70239 of the 56th FG HQ, Boxted, April 1945

55
P-47M-1 44-21212 of the 61st FS, Boxted, April 1945

56
P-47M-1 44-21112 of Maj George Bostwick, CO of the 63rd FS, Boxted, April 1945

57
P-47M-1 44-21141/'the Brat' of Lt Randell Murphy, 63rd FS, Boxted, April 1945

58
He 111H-23 Wk-Nr 701152 of the 61st FS, Boxted, July 1945

1
56th Fighter Group

2
61st Fighter Squadron

3
62nd Fighter Squadron

4
63rd Fighter Squadron

weather kept the bombers on the ground for a spell. During this time a new P-47 model with significant improvements arrived at Boxted. The main feature was a reduction in rear fuselage height and a 'bubble canopy' over the cockpit, which gave the pilot all-round vision. Strangely, the new model was still identified as a P-47D, distinguished from earlier models by the production block number -25-RE. But among other changes, the internal tankage had been boosted by another 65 US gallons, which would allow for a greater radius of action. The oxygen supply and water for engine injection had also been increased.

The first of what the group dubbed 'Superbolts' went to the CO, who used it to lead a bomber support mission on the 19th when five more destroyed claims were made. The next four 'Superbolts' were allotted to Schilling, who had recently returned from US leave, and the three squadron COs, Gabreski, Dade and Goodfleisch. Unfortunately, the extra range potential of the new model could not be realised while the majority of the group's aircraft were the older models.

It was soon discovered that the 'Superbolt' was not as laterally stable as its forerunners, requiring more pilot attention – removal of the high spine behind the cockpit was a contributing factor. The D-25s arrived without camouflage finish, as had most new P-47s received from mid-April, following a decision by the USAAF to save production cost and time, in addition to reducing aircraft weight.

A pre-flighting engine fire claimed Mike Gladych's *PENGIE III* P-47D 42-26300/HV-V on 18 July 1944. Gladych scored one victory in this aircraft, on D-Day. His final tally with the 56th FG was ten destroyed in the air and eight on the ground, to which he could add eight destroyed in the air, two probables and a solitary shared damage claim during three years of frontline flying with the RAF

However, VIII Fighter Command advised the groups to add some form of camouflage to the upper surfaces of these all-metal finish fighters, for there was a likelihood that they might have to operate from continental bases following a successful invasion, and Luftwaffe attacks on battlefront airfields could be expected. Thus, P-47s of the 56th FG began to appear with a wide variety of camouflage schemes and colours – yet another example of this group markedly distinguishing itself from the other 14 in VIII Fighter Command, who generally kept to a coat of dark green paint.

On 22 May the group CO set off from Boxted with 48 P-47s to try an improved 'Zemke Fan', this time going to the 'Happy Hunting Ground'. At Dümmer Lake the group spread, this time at 16-aeroplane squadron strength in battle formation. East of Bremen the 61st FS observed Fw 190s taking off from an airfield, so Gabreski took his squadron down to engage at a few thousand feet. In the combat that ensued 'Gabby' downed two fighters, but two members of his flight fell to the enemy. One, 2Lt Richard Heineman, had claimed his first air victory just three days earlier.

In further action in the same vicinity, Gabreski made another kill to boost the 61st's mission tally to 11. Another P-47 was badly shot up in the fight, but pilot McMinn managed to nurse his aircraft back to crash-land at Leiston. Yet another pilot, Lt Billy Edens, had a lucky escape when he was forced to ditch in the sea after running out of fuel. Escapes from single-engine fighters put into the sea were rare, but Edens survived and was rescued from his dinghy.

Later that day Zemke led 24 P-47s with a 500-lb bomb on each wing rack to experiment on the most effective way to dive-bomb a bridge. The target selected was at Hasselt, in the Netherlands. Diving at various angles from heights of 15,000, 10,000 and 12,000 ft, none of the bombs demolished the bridge, and as to what constituted the best form of attack

The first 'silver' P-47D in the 61st FS was 42-26044/HV-Z, which became Capt James Carter's assigned aircraft and carried the name *Silver Lady*. Carter made only one of his seven (six confirmed) aerial claims with this aircraft, although other pilots used it to shoot down another ten enemy fighters – Gabreski got five of these and Gladych two. Seen here with crew chief Sgt Joe Gibson, Jim Carter was an original combat pilot of the 61st FS, and rose to command the squadron during his second tour

Lt Steve Gerick tucks in tightly
during a formation banking turn over
Essex in his P-47D 42-26024/HV-O in
July 1944. Although 56th wartime
credits gave Gerick just five air and
two ground victories, plus nine
damaged claims, his aircraft carries
ten victory symbols – with the
exception of one Fw 190, all marked
as 'ME 109s'. Gerick served with the
group from December 1943 through
to late June 1944, when he
transferred to the 495th FTG at
Atcham, in Shropshire

remained unresolved. Other dive-bombing raids were carried out during
following days, when it was concluded that approaches from altitudes
between 12,000 and 10,000 ft, with a 5000-ft dive at an angle around 75
degrees, was the most effective for accuracy.

With a cross-Channel invasion imminent, and an upsurge in fighter-
bombing activity, the 56th tried another high-level bombing experiment,
this time using a P-38J 'Droop Snoot' – a theatre modification whereby
the nose armament of a P-38 Lightning was removed and a compartment,
complete with transparency, fashioned for a bombardier and Norden
bombsight. Zemke borrowed one from the 20th FG, and on 30 May set
off leading 16 P-47s (each carrying two 1000-lb bombs) to attack a rail
bridge near Criel from 12,000 ft. An intense flak barrage greeted them, so
Zemke decided to attack another bridge some five miles to the south at
Chattily, where three spans were taken out. Even so, it was decided that
any future attacks using this method should employ 500-lb bombs, as the
P-47's wing loading with 'thousand pounders' made handling tricky, particularly on take-off and when trying to keep formation. The 20th FG
wanted their 'Droop Snoot', back so the 56th had to return to dive- and
glide-bombing.

It was very evident from all the military and naval activity observed from
the air that the long heralded cross-Channel invasion of the European
continent was near. Fighter-bombing missions became more frequent,

83

and in early June were concentrated in, and around, the Pas de Calais area as part of the deception plan to make the enemy believe this was where the landings would be made. After leading an uneventful Type 16 patrol during the morning of 5 June, Zemke was called to 'Ajax', where along with the other VIII Fighter Command group commanders he was briefed on their participation in Operation *Overlord*.

Back at Boxted, strict security was enforced, with visitors detained for the night without explanation and all local telephone connections temporarily suspended. When orders were given for the groundcrews to paint alternating black and white stripes on wings and fuselage, there was general speculative agreement on what was pending.

The first mission of D-Day – to patrol north of the landing areas – was launched at 0336 hours. Led by Gabreski, 32 P-47s took off with navigation lights glowing to add to the vast spectacle of reds, greens and whites that already filled the night sky. Although strong enemy reaction was expected, the Luftwaffe was conspicuous by its absence, and little was seen of the enemy on this and most of the eight missions undertaken that day, four of which were fighter-bombing tasks.

An Fw 190 was claimed on the fifth outing by a 62nd FS pilot, and on the final mission Mike Gladych, the itinerant Pole, brought down a Bf 109 (his 13th victory, and fifth with the USAAF), while Zemke's interception of another caused its pilot to lose control and crash. The group's only loss on D-Day was five-victory ace Evan McMinn, who was killed

The ETO's top scoring US air ace, Lt Col Francis Gabreski, vacates his P-47D 42-26418/HV-A at Boxted after leading the 61st FS on a top cover mission in support of a fighter-bomber raid on 15 July 1944. His full tally of 28 aerial victories can be seen below the cockpit of the fighter, Gabreski having claimed his last kill (a Bf 109) on 5 July. Just five days after this photograph was taken, Gabreski struck the ground with 42-26418's propeller while strafing He 111s at Bassinheim airfield. Managing to clear the airfield, 'Gabby' successfully bellied the aircraft into a nearby field and was quickly captured. One of the first 'bubble canopy' Thunderbolts to arrive at Boxted, this aircraft was flown in a natural metal finish for several missions prior to being camouflaged

Two 63rd FS Thunderbolts lift off from Boxted's runway 28 for a fighter-bomber mission on the afternoon of 15 July 1944. They are carry 500-lb GP bombs on the wing racks and a 108-US gallon tank under the fuselage

when shot down by ground fire while strafing north-east of Bernay. Eight fighter-bomber missions were flown the following day, and of the five P-47s that failed to return, three fell to ground fire, one was caught in the explosion of an ordnance-filled rail wagon being dive-bombed and the fifth was believed to have been shot down by enemy fighters. Three pilots were killed and two evaded capture.

The Luftwaffe did appear on this day, and the 56th's squadrons were able to make surprise attacks on low-flying Bf 109s and Fw 190s, with destroyed claims of 12. On the other hand, the P-47s were also vulnerable to bounces at low altitude, and while the Thunderbolt's robustness withstood many cannon shell and bullet strikes, several aircraft returned badly damaged. Water injection greatly aided performance at low altitude, but the P-47 was still slow to accelerate.

During the penultimate mission of the day the group CO accounted for two Fw 190s caught near Nantes. Back at Boxted he found one of the RAF Polish volunteers, Flt Lt Zbigniew Janicki, orbiting in an effort to get his P-47's landing gear to come down. For a while Zemke flew alongside in his D-25, advising Janicki on manoeuvres, but all to no avail – cannon shell hits in an air fight had apparently jammed the release mechanism. Finally, Janicki 'bellied in' his Thunderbolt on an out of use runway, and despite a shower of sparks, the P-47 did not catch fire. Six days later Janicki lost his life in unknown circumstances during a fighter-bomber mission, being the only one of seven Poles flying with the 56th to perish.

85

COMBAT REPORT

'Hub' Zemke often said that only about one in ten fighter pilots shot down ever saw their assailant. Personal experience endorsed this maxim, particularly on the early evening mission of 7 June 1944, the day following the launch of the cross-Channel invasion;

'After the squadron made its bombing run, we wandered south-west in the quest of enemy road and rail activities, or to engage any enemy aircraft that could be found. As we flew over Mantes-Gassicourt, France, I looked down from 10,000 ft and thought I saw a truck convoy on the road just north of the Seine River. I led the squadron across the river and did a 180-degree turn to return, in the meantime ordering the lower six aircraft of my immediate support to follow me down to investigate the convoy. Lt Rankin was told to circle aloft at 14,000 ft and give us cover. The convoy proved to be piles of brown stones piled along the road, so we pulled up and climbed back through a cloud level just above. Just as we broke out of the top of the cloud level, Lt Rankin, in the top cover, reported three enemy aircraft climbing rapidly above the cloud level, then he said many bandits coming up.

'We were hit from above by approximately 15 Fw 190s and Me 109s, everyone breaking into them as fast as possible. I shot at two Fw 190s above with considerable deflection, more to make them break than to hit them, and immediately wheeled to the left to get out of the fire of an enemy Me 109, who was firing to beat hell. He passed in back of me from his 90-degree side approach and continued straight away, never waiting to turn back or recover.

'Six aircraft were immediately picked up two or three miles to the west and above, so I continued to hold everything forward and climb in their direction. My difference in altitude and the distance that separated us caused me to lose some distance but I gained altitude. Somewhere past Evreaux airdrome, I could only see two some ten miles ahead of me. These two did an abrupt turn to the south-east and started to fly south-east toward Paris. Again I picked up all six of them. The four leading were five miles ahead. At a point over Dreux airdrome I bounced the two stragglers from 22,000 ft, only to discover they were two of my own outfit chasing the Hun. I gave them orders to join up with me as I was by myself, and we would pursue the four ahead. The two misinterpreted and probably due to the shortage of gas turned and went home.

'The enemy, who were only specks toward Paris by now, were slowly climbing so I thought, "Here's a beautiful chance for a sneak kill". Again the throttle was boosted and I pointed the ship upwards. South of Paris, the four Fws did a right turn to head west, enabling me to cut off considerable distance. My altitude was about 27,000 ft, theirs being approximately 20,000 ft. Again somewhere over Chartres, they conveniently did a 180-degree turn and headed east. This last turn put me almost directly over them, and the attack was started. All flew in a company front as we do. As I drew to a point approximately 2000 yards in the rear of the four, the leader did a 45-degree turn to the south-east and everyone began to cross over. I picked out the last

---

The cloud cover that had obscured the invasion area during the first two days was worse on 8 June, and only two operations were undertaken, one of which was a bomber escort. The next day the overcast was so extensive no missions were attempted. The weather had improved sufficiently on the 10th for three fighter-bomber missions, with one aircraft falling victim to flak, although the pilot escaped. Ground support missions predominated during the rest of the month, and when there was support for the heavy bombers, it brought little contact with the Luftwaffe – P-51-equipped groups continued to make headlines when it came to air battles.

Since D-Day Francis Gabreski had been credited with four victories, and on 27 June a fifth took his total of credits to 27 to tie him with Bob Johnson (who had finished his tour) as the leading ace in the ETO.

July followed the pattern of June, with ground support missions predominating, but it opened well, for on Independence Day the 56th was

Fw 190 and opened up on a 20-degree deflection shot, hitting him squarely after about 50 rounds. He went off spinning in flame, straight for the earth.

'The remaining three completed the turn and flew a three-airplane company front. The element leader was picked out next, with me flying about 300-400 yards to the rear. I opened up on him from directly astern, flying straight and level. It is definitely recalled that he rocked his wings and I would rock my wings in return. He probably thought I was his wingman, who I had just shot down in the cross over turn, and was saying over the R/T: "Hans, you bastard, move up in line abreast and stop flying in back of me". At any rate, I fired and fired at this pilot to finally tag him with a decent concentration, and he nosed over to go straight down.

'This left two Fws still flying line abreast and unconcerned, so I slid over in back of the Flight Leader and opened fire. My tracers showed just as I hit him and the jinx was up, for he immediately began kicking rudder to roll over on his back and I swung over on the last man to shoot at him as he went down. No hits were seen, but I claim a damage against the Flight Leader. Both were seen running like mad in a steep dive, so I climbed up to 29,000 ft and came screaming home. The combat was at 22,000-24,000 ft. I claim two Fw 190s destroyed and one Fw 190 damaged.'

A few days later the colonel submitted another report;

'Upon return of my combat film for 7 June 1944, on which I claimed to have attacked four Fw 190s to destroy two of them and damaged the third, it has been found that a malfunction of the gun camera exposed all the film before the combat. Therefore no aircraft are shown.

'The mission of that day took us to Gourney, France, where I selected the small marshalling yards as the group dive-bombing target. The guns were fired in the dive as I normally do and through a short in the extra jump wire, the entire film was exposed, though I fired only one burst of 25 rounds. Later, when I snuck in back of four Fw 190s south-west of Paris, there was no film to confirm my strikes. All of my shots were, incidentally, directly from astern, and would have shown the enemy aircraft. As the two pilots who accompanied me in pursuit of the enemy had to return home before the action, there was no visual confirmation.

'Upon returning to base I immediately had my film packet checked for exposure and the armament men told me it had been completely exposed. This seemed strange for it is not usually the case to use all the film when firing just a bit over 200 rounds of ammunition from each gun. I, therefore, told them to check the camera installation.

'Not until the return of the exposed film did anyone inform me that there had been camera trouble. As soon as I inquired, the armament section of the particular squadron confessed they had never made a definite check of the wiring on my aircraft until this malfunction. Their investigation on the evening of the 7 June revealed that a secondary jump wire had shorted out the camera to expose all the film. The wrath of a CO descended about them.

'As to my confirmations, I therefore request them withdrawn, and hope to prove my claim after the war if the Germans keep a file.'

able to claim 20 aerial victories (later reassessed as 17), which took the group past the 500 destroyed mark – another first for the USAAF in Europe. It was just like old times when, for the second day running, the group again showed its prowess in combat with the Luftwaffe on the 5th.

Tasked to meet B-17s returning from the first Russia shuttle mission via way of Italy, a formation of Bf 109s and Fw 190s was encountered near Evreux, and in the ensuing battle 11 of the enemy were claimed for the loss of one. Gabreski duly shot down a Bf 109 for his 28th victory, thus making him the leading Eighth Air Force ace. This total was never surpassed by any other American pilot flying against the Luftwaffe.

The air action continued the next day when a fighter-bomber mission was bounced by Bf 109s near Bernay. The 56th pilots turned to meet the attack, but one P-47 was shot down. In the ensuing action one enemy aircraft was seen to disintegrate, presumably through airframe or engine fail-

A flight peel off on return from the afternoon mission of 15 July 1944. Lt Col David Schilling's P-47D stands in the foreground, and another Thunderbolt can be seen below its left wing on its landing approach to the main Boxted runway

Another 56th innovation – 'Hub' Zemke had a K-25 camera fixed to the seat armour plate of his aircraft to enable him to take oblique photographs of ground targets. This frame shows a freight train after it had been shot up south-east of Paris on 16 July 1944. Two locomotives and a number of rail cars were set on fire. This camera fitment was soon adopted by other groups as well

ure, while another, struck by a jettisoned 150-US gallon metal fuel tank, lost a wing. This unusual happening was the result of 1Lt Joe Curtis forgetting to release his belly tank until entering a turn with a pursuing Messerschmitt. The group claimed five aerial victories on this day, and the winning streak continued on the 7th when a further ten enemy aircraft were shot down during a Ramrod for bombers raiding Leipzig. All were Junkers Ju 52/3m transports caught orbiting Gardelegen airfield, where Capt Fred Christensen had taken the 62nd FS down to strafe dispersed aircraft.

Christensen himself shot down six of the helpless transports, which elevated his personal total of victories to 21 and one shared. From there on the enemy was again rarely seen in the sky, and nearly four weeks would pass before Zemke's wingman, 2Lt Richard Anderson, broke the void by shooting down an Fw 190 that went after the CO when he was concentrating on strafing a train.

In mid-July Dave Schilling and the other pilots who had been on leave in the USA returned to the group. Capt Joe Egan replaced Maj Goodfleisch as CO of the 63rd, 'Goodie', who had completed over 300 operational hours, being due to return to the States on leave. On 19 July (just two days after receiving this appointment), Egan was killed when he flew into electric cables while strafing north-east of Nancy. The following day the 61st FS lost its commander.

Fred Christensen's P-47D 42-26628/ LM-C *Rozzi Geth II* was unusual in that it carried the ace's 22 victory symbols on both sides of the fuselage, as well as the crew panel. Photographed on a warm July day, one of the Boxted domestic sites can be seen in the distance under the right wing

COMBAT REPORT

The fate of three enemy aircraft on the morning 6 July 1944 was unusual, as recounted in the following combat reports. The 62nd FS was flying top cover for the other squadrons carrying bombs, the action taking place near Beaumont, France, in a cloudless sky with slight haze. The combat report lodged by 1Lt George E Bostwick of the 62nd FS is recounted first;

'I was leading the second element of White Flight at 14,000 ft when we spotted some 40-plus enemy aircraft above at 20,000 to 25,000 ft. White Leader (Col Zemke) threw everything forward and started towards them in a 180-degree turn. At about 19,000 ft we were bounced by two Me 109s in head-on passes. They had just passed under us when another Me 109 slid in on Col Zemke's tail, who in turn broke to the right and requested assistance. I gave my aircraft water and closed to within 300/400 yards of the Jerry who, by this time, was within 75/100 yards of Col Zemke. As I opened fire on the enemy aircraft he did a tumbling roll and then split-S'd. I did the same and followed him through two rolls to the left, going straight down and firing short bursts, for I was in a good position and range. As the Jerry straight-ened out and dove vertically for the deck, I hit compressibility and the enemy aircraft, apparently, did likewise. My aircraft slowly straightened out at 7000 to 8000 ft and, for a minute, it seemed that the Jerry would, too. He never quite made it, though, and crashed into the ground at about a 45-degree angle. I then circled at 1000 ft, cleared my tail and went down and took pictures of the enemy aircraft.'

Supporting statement from Col Zemke;

'Leading the White section of the 62nd FS, we encountered a large gaggle of enemy aircraft over Bernay. Pulling up in a steep all out climb toward the enemy, I was followed by the 62nd Squadron. Two Me 109s passed directly over me and I continued on, expecting my following flight to take care of them. One of these must have rolled over on my tail, for shortly afterwards I saw tracers zipping past me. Looking back, there was an Me 109 not more than 150 yards distance in back of me, blazing away. A steep right turn was entered and a call for my wingman to take this bastard off my tail. At that point I saw a P-47 shooting at fairly long range at the Me 109. Since the time was passing too fast without

---

After performing escort duties for B-17s, 'Gabby' Gabreski led his squadron in strafing a number of He 111s spotted on an airfield at Bassenheim. Allied fighter pilots undertaking strafing runs had quickly realised that the lower the pass across enemy airfields the more difficult it was for the defending gunners to target them. However, on this occasion Gabreski flew too low, striking the ground with the propeller of his Thunderbolt (P-47D-25 42-26418/HV-A). Managing to clear the airfield, 'Gabby' successfully bellied the aircraft into a nearby field. The USAAF's leading ace in the ETO saw out the rest of the conflict as a PoW – he had been scheduled to return to the US, having reached the 300-hour mark.

Gabreski's replacement as 61st CO was Maj Gordon Baker, who had only joined the 56th in June. Harold Comstock, who had returned from Stateside leave at the same time as Schilling and Egan, was given command of the 63rd.

The ever active Zemke had again turned his attention to medium level formation bombing using a 'Droop Snoot' P-38 and bombardier to sight on the target. A suitably-modified Lightning was duly acquired from the 55th FG, which was then converting to Mustangs. With the aircraft painted up in 56th FG colours, on the afternoon of 25 July 'The Hub' set off with Lt Scroggins in the 'Droop Snoot', the P-38 carrying two 500-lb bombs under each wing. The intention was to bomb an enemy aircraft he had seen being hidden on Montdidier airfield earlier in the day.

Target for Tonight was P-47D 42-25721/UN-P, which carried a female motif based on well known Vargas calendar artwork. Lt Sam Lowman was killed in this aircraft when the 63rd FS was bounced by Bf 109s near Bernay during a fighter-bomber mission on 7 July 1944

results, I started to flick in an aileron roll straight down just as the enemy aircraft registered a hit on my left wing, which blew the ammunition door open. On recovery from about a half-turn of a roll straight down, I looked down to see the Me 109 being pursued by a P-47 with all guns blazing. The attitude of both aircraft being about straight down, I thought at that moment "You two sports better pull out or you'll hit the ground". Since my aircraft hardly flew normal without trim, and the open ammunition door kept pounding my wing, I moved off home. The Me 109 was not seen to crash, but I feel that the P-47 pilot had a wonderful position to polish him off when I last saw the two.'

Meanwhile the 63rd FS was being bounced. The destruction of the enemy aircraft mentioned in 1Lt Joseph R Curtis's report was witnessed by several other pilots;

'I was flying number 3 in Daily Yellow flight, consisting of Lts Ross, Warboys, myself and F/O Magel. We made landfall in at 0600 hours just west of Dieppe at 10,000 ft, and continued on course until we reached an altitude of about 14,000 ft. Daily Blue Leader called in some bogies above and behind us. These turned out to be about 40-plus Me 109s. They positioned themselves on us and started to

bounce. Four of the superior number were making an attack on our flight. They were flying line abreast and pulling heavy black smoke during their descent. About halfway down on the attack one of the 109s exploded in mid-air. This was no doubt caused by excessive manifold pressure in his steep dive. Daily Yellow Flight is claiming this airplane as destroyed, shared by the four of us.

'After we had jettisoned our bombs we had to make several breaks into the enemy aircraft. The last break that I participated in ended up with two Me 109s on my tail and six more giving the two top cover. We had completed two turns when I realised that I still had my external tank. I immediately released the tank, which gave me a much shorter turning radius. By some freak accident my external tank hit the second Me 109 and tore about half of his left wing off. I think the tank exploded when it hit the wing. I last saw the Me 109 in a steep spiral to the left. All this time I was still turning with the other 109. I made 20 plus turns with the 109 on my tail, and luckily he never did score a hit on me. The other six Me 109s had disappeared when we finished our turning. I do not know how or what happened to my friend, the 109. After our show today I think the Thunderbolt is the best airplane flying in this combat theatre today.'

A dozen 'bubble top' P-47Ds of the 62nd FS are seen on a routine training flight. Led by bare metal finish LM-Q, each flight is stacked down to enable pilots to comfortably hold position

The groundcrew often had to work in the most inclement conditions to maintain their charges. They knew that any failure on their part might cost a pilot his life. S/Sgt Joe Brennan looked after Lt George Bostwick's P-47D 42-26280/LM-Z during the summer of 1944. None of Bostwick's eight aerial victories were claimed in this particular aircraft. Polishing the outer surfaces could provide that fraction of extra performance in combat that could save the pilot's life

Trailing a P-47 formation led by Schilling, which was heading for a suspected Wehrmacht store hidden in a French forest, Zemke broke away to bomb Montdidier from 12,000 ft. Scroggins had just released the bombs when a direct flak hit completely severed the starboard propeller and engine reduction gearing, momentarily causing Zemke to loose control. The 'Droop Snoot' was successfully nursed back to Boxted, where an emergency landing was carried out. This incident was enough to deter 'Hub' from future experiments of this nature.

Dive-bombing missions in support of the advancing ground forces continued to occupy the group during August 1944, and where escorts and support of the heavy bombers was called for, no aerial opposition was encountered. The Luftwaffe opposition to the B-17s and B-24s was now usually found beyond the range of the P-47 groups where the P-51s continued to see most of the action.

Since the early spring a marked deterioration in the general quality of Luftwaffe fighter pilots had been apparent, and this had reached the point where Mustang pilots often returned from long missions with individuals claiming multiple victories – even as many as five or six. A crisis in Luftwaffe fighter pilot training was evident, and this became even more apparent as the days passed. The aggressive Zemke was frustrated to see the Mustang groups taking all the honours.

James, the third McClure pilot to serve with the 62nd FS, was a star turn on a unicycle. He was yet another replacement pilot who never had an opportunity to shoot down an enemy aircraft, despite flying 63 missions. The P-47D in the background is 42-26298/LM-<u>A</u> *Stalag Luft III/I Wanted Wings*, assigned to Lt Albert Knafelz

Glenn Miller (left) arrived in a Liberator to play in No 1 hangar at Boxted on 6 August 1944. His welcoming committee included, from left to right, 1Lt A L Mellor (Special Services Officer who accompanied Miller on his tour), Lt Col David Schilling and Lt Col Douglas Pollard (CO of the 33rd Service Group, which supported the 56th FG)

Capt Don Smith's *"OLE' COCK III"* 42-28382/HV-S is seen with rocket tubes installed under the wings in August 1944. At the time, this aircraft sported the most distinctive markings of any P-47D at Boxted, being painted in light sky blue undersides, a two-shade grey camouflage on the upper surfaces and black letters with a white outline. Smith claimed 5.5 aerial kills, 1 probable and two damaged during his tour in the ETO, the last of these being downed on 22 February 1944

On the afternoon of 11 August he received a phone call from Gen Griswold of VIII Fighter Command, who requested that David Schilling go to Wattisham to take command of the 479th FG, whose CO (Col Kyle L Riddle) had just been shot down. Schilling was not enthusiastic about leaving the 56th, so Zemke volunteered in his place, eager to accept the challenge of leading the youngest of the Command's 15 groups, which was due to convert from P-38s to P-51s. It came as a shock to the men at Boxted that the man who had been synonymous with the 56th should decide to leave them.

However, Dave Schilling was a popular and respected leader, and with the help of the other old hands, maintained the established *esprit de corps*. Zemke's move was also occasioned by his knowing that high command wanted to retire him to a desk – a fate he was determined to avoid if at all possible. On 30 October a storm tore his P-51D (44-14351/9B-Z) apart, and he saw the war out as the Senior Allied Officer at *Stalag Luft 1*. 'Hub' Zemke's final wartime tally was 17.75 aircraft shot down, 2 probables, 9 damaged and 6.6 destroyed on the ground.

Schilling made Maj Lucien 'Pete' Dade his deputy, and elevated Capt Mike Quirk to command the 62nd FS in Dade's place. Quirk was another 'original', with 12 air and 7 ground strafing kills to his credit. Schilling first took the group out as its CO on 12 August, leading one of two A and B dive-bombing missions flown that day against enemy transportation.

Pilots may have come and gone but groundcrews remained the constant within the fighter groups in the ETO. For example, Capt Townsend Parsons was the fourth pilot assigned an aircraft in the hands of S/Sgt Carl Conner and his crew – Conner had previously looked after Fred Christensen's LM-C. *Barbara B* was P-47D 42-28806/LM-C, and it was eventually lost to flak, along with its pilot, Flt Off Alben Calmes, on 30 November 1944

Support of the ground forces continued to be the group's main occupation for the rest of August as the Wehrmacht retreated from France. Air-launched rocket projectiles were made available to VIII Fighter Command P-47 groups at this time, and the 56th was the first to try them operationally. Lt Col Schilling and Mike Quirk gave the weapon its front-line debut with the group, having three-cluster launch tubes installed under each wing. These were in turn used during a dive-bombing attack by the 56th on the marshalling yards at Braine le Comte.

The rockets proved difficult to aim and their tracks erratic. Schilling led more rocket-armed P-47s back to the same target three days later with no better success – if there was a technique in the accurate aim of this weapon it was not easily acquired. After a further unsatisfactory effort to master aiming the weapon this, plus the drag of the tubes and its effect on handling, resulted in a decision to discontinue the use of rockets. Another 'first in the ETO' for the 56th occurred on 18 August when so-called spike bombs were used. This blast weapon had an 18-inch by $2^{1}/_{2}$-inch metal spike in the nose so that it detonated above the surface of the ground.

The group now had sufficient numbers of long-ranged D-25 'Super-bolt' models to venture further afield on ground attack missions. On one such mission to the Saarbrucken area on 28 August, a number of low flying enemy aircraft were surprised and six shot down. On 5 September two strafing sweeps of German airfields resulted in eight air victories without loss and a record 78 aircraft destroyed and 19 damaged on the ground in the Koblenz-Frankfurt area for the loss of four P-47s – one pilot was killed, one made prisoner and two evaded capture.

Deeper penetrations could now also be made, as in the event of diminishing fuel supply the Thunderbolts could put down on airstrips in liberated France. These were also a haven for badly damaged aircraft that might

This photograph was taken by Capt Comstock with a K-25 camera fixed to the armour plate of P-47D-25-RE 42-26413/UN-Z. It shows smoke rising from burning aircraft at Gelnhausen airfield on 5 September 1944

otherwise not have made it home to Boxted. The group still expected to be moved to an airfield on the Continent, which would greatly facilitate endurance over enemy held territory. To this end, the programme of applying camouflage to the upper surfaces of the unpainted P-47s was continued, although there always remained several 'silver' aircraft on group strength.

The 56th's individuality was promoted by the display of paint schemes ranging from disruptive patterns of greens and greys, blotchings in greens and greys, to all black or all green. In September the 63rd FS commenced painting the rudders of its aircraft blue, and later the 56th's scheme of identifying its squadrons with different-coloured rudders was officially taken up by the Eighth Air Force for all its fighter squadrons.

COMBAT REPORT

On 5 September 1944 the 56th FG came home from a strafing sweep with claims of 78 enemy aircraft destroyed and 19 damaged on airfields in western Germany. Lt Col David Schilling reported his part in this then record bag as follows;

'I was leading the 63rd Squadron, and when we reached Gelnhausen airdrome, I told my Red and Blue Flights to orbit the field while I took my flight across the field to draw out any flak that might be around. On our first pass, we came across the field from the east to the west along the south side of the airdrome. My No 2 man and I were the only ones to fire on this pass, silencing flak positions on the east side of the field on the way in. I also fired at two Fw 190s located near the south-east corner of the field, and raked my fire through a blister hangar near the centre of the south side of the field, as I strafed the whole south side.

Lt Rotzeler, my wingman, also strafed the entire length of the field, damaging some Fw 190s which were lined up just in front of the hangar on the west side of the airdrome. The flight then dropped down to the deck and pulled up about two miles from the field.

'The flight's second pass was made in the same direction over the southern hangar line. Lt Rotzeler destroyed an Fw 190 camouflaged under a tree, and Lt Albright blew up a Ju 52 in flames in the south-east corner.

'The third and fourth passes were made the same as the second. This time I destroyed an Fw 190 east of the large hangar near the south-west side. Lt Rotzler destroyed an Fw 190 and Lt Danial destroyed an Fw 190 in the same area.

'I then called in that the flights should change their direction of attack due to the smoke and the availability of targets, and to come in from the south to the north along the west side of the field. Three passes were made in this direction by my flight.

'On my sixth pass I saw two planes in the hangar near the south-west corner on the south side of the field and concentrated on them. Lt Albright spotted another one in the hangar and destroyed it. The hangar burst into flames from my attack and burnt to the ground, destroying everything in it. Lt Rotzler destroyed an Fw 190 in the south-west corner on his fifth pass. On his sixth pass he suspected flak firing from the hangar on the west side of the field. Raking his fire down the entire length of the building, he scored many hits on the planes inside. On his seventh pass, Lt Rotzler destroyed what he believed to be an Me 109 on the north side of the field.'

On the way back to base, following the attack on Gelnhausen airfield, Col Schilling called in that he could see an Fw 190 flying down the Rhine. He asked someone to make the attack as he was out of ammunition. Lt Timony, Blue Leader, spotted the enemy aircraft at about 4000 ft below him at 2 o'clock. Moving in on the Focke Wulf from its left and rear, Timony opened fire at about 400 yards and closed to 100 yards before observing hits on the left wing root and across the nose;

'I was forced to break off firing and slid up beside the enemy aircraft while he released his canopy, climbed out of the cockpit and slide off his left wing.'

The Fw 190 crashed and exploded in some woods on the east side of the Rhine about 15 miles south of Koblenz.

MARKET AND THE '**BULGE**'

Ground attack continued to claim its victims within the 56th FG as summer turned to autumn. Some 18 pilots were posted Missing In Action from this activity in September alone, although seven survived as prisoners or evaded capture. On 10 September the 62nd's CO, Mike Quirk, and last of the squadron's originals, fell to flak, but he managed to bail out successfully and was made a PoW – likewise, 1Lt Billy Edens, who had joined the squadron as a replacement in April 1944, and had quickly scored seven victories between 8 June and 7 July. Maj Les Smith (another group original, who also finished the war with seven aerial victories) was transferred from the 61st to replace Quirk. But worst was to come eight days later. In fact 18 September turned out to be the blackest day ever for the group.

On the 17th the Allies had launched the audacious airborne invasion of the Netherlands, codenamed Operation *Market*. The 56th, along with the remaining three P-47 groups of the Eighth Air Force and some from the Ninth, were given the task of going after transportation targets to hinder enemy reinforcement, as well as the far more hazardous job of identifying and attacking enemy anti-aircraft positions to lessen the flak facing the lumbering transport aircraft stuffed full of paratroopers and equipment. Cloud and haze made it difficult to locate the targets, but flak claimed one P-47 with its pilot and wounded two others, both of whom managed to fly back to England where one had to bail out.

Capt Michael Jackson's P-47D 44-19780/LM-J *Teddy* **was photographed whilst being worked on outside No 2 hangar at Boxted on 11 October 1944. Jackson had four air and four ground victories to his credit at the time this shot was taken, and he had increased these tallies to 8 and 5.5 respectively by the end of his tour**

Following P-47D 42-75276/LM-**M**'s retirement as war weary in August 1944, 56th FG groundcrews modified the fighter so that a passenger could be carried behind the pilot. The work involved in re-positioning the radio and oxygen equipment, cutting into the fuselage, adding stress members and fashioning a sliding canopy that would give access to both crew positions was largely carried out by S/Sgts Thurman Schreel and Charles Taylor of the 41st Service Squadron. Their creation was unofficially known as the 'Doublebolt' within the 56th, and it made its first post-modification flight on 10 September 1944. The aircraft was subsequently used primarily in the liaison role, although groundcrews occasionally got to ride in it too. In April 1945, following fitment of Rosebud search radar, 42-75276 participated in a further four combat missions

The next day's mission again called for much 'flak busting' to support B-24s re-supplying the paratroopers. 'Bunny' Comstock headed the formations tasked with this duty in the Turnhout area of Holland. The weather was worse than the previous day, with cloud down to 500 ft and haze hindering visibility so that it was difficult to spot enemy gun positions until they opened fire. In any case, Allied fighters had been briefed not to shoot at ground targets until fired upon to avoid mistakenly attacking friendly forces.

Of the 39 P-47s despatched, only 23 returned to Boxted that afternoon, 12 of them with various degrees of shell and bullet damage. The fate of the missing 16 was not fully resolved for some days. Nine pilots had safely crash-landed or bailed out in Allied occupied territory, whilst a tenth, whose aircraft was shot up by friendly groundfire, landed at RAF airstrip B.52 on the continent. Another attempting to return to Boxted crashed fatally on mud flats in Bradwell Bay, and the remaining five went down in enemy occupied territory, of which three survived as prisoners.

Despite these staggering losses there was no respite for the group, and next day Schilling took 32 of his Thunderbolts on an uneventful bomber escort. On the 20th it was back to dive-bombing and flak busting in the Arnhem area, but only one P-47 sustained substantial flak damage and its pilot managed to bring it back to the 'crash' airfield at Manston. At a later date the group was awarded another DUC for its work on 18 September.

If group morale had taken a knock on the 18th, it was elevated three days later. Tasked with giving area support to RAF Stirlings and Dakotas reinforcing the beleaguered airborne forces, the 56th had to operate at lower altitudes than normal for escort duties. While flying south between Deventer and Lochem, a loose formation of some 15 Fw 190s was spotted

at a few hundred feet, headed east from the battle area. With altitude advantage and apparent surprise, the 'Wolfpack' descended on the enemy aircraft and proceeded to claim all 15 destroyed in a furious engagement which lasted just a few minutes, and saw two 63rd FS aircraft failing to return. Dave Schilling, leading the group, was responsible for downing three of the enemy fighters, raising his personal tally to 17 aerial victories.

Towards the end of the September Maj Dade was granted permission to return to the US due to a family bereavement, and his place as Deputy Group Commander and Flying Executive was vtaken by Gordon Baker, who turned over the 61st FS to Donovan Smith. From 15 September the 65th FW (and its five groups) was transferred from VIII Fighter Command to the 2nd Bomb Division (BD), which in effect turned each of the three divisions into air forces within the Eighth Air Force.

The transfer of Fighter Command staff and the issue of Field Orders by division took some time to complete, but it meant that in future the 56th would predominately be shepherding B-24 Liberators. Following the successes of 21 September, a total of 33 missions would be flown before the Luftwaffe was engaged in another extensive, and fruitful, battle. During October just one enemy aircraft fell to 56th guns, and a few others were seen. The Luftwaffe had now taken to harbouring its forces for large-scale forays against the day bombers, so even the long-legged Mustangs often found little opposition.

The battle lines in western Europe now placed much enemy-held territory beyond the economical range of P-47 bombing missions, and the

There was never a shortage of work for mechanics in the ETO. P-47D 42-25261/UN-I is seen under repair outside No 1 hangar at Boxted in the early winter of 1944. Note the specially-modified GMC 'deuce-and-a-half' truck, which has been fitted with a hoist for lifting heavy loads such as bombs, fuel tanks or engines. The '6 x 6' – officially designated the CCKW 353 (long) or CCKW 352 (short) by GMC – was assigned to the 33rd Service Group

Ninth Air Force provided most of the needed ground support. But this did not preclude the 56th from occasionally bombing and strafing airfields in Germany, and other targets of opportunity, where flak frequently exacted a toll. Ramrods predominated during the autumn and early winter, yet time and again no aerial opposition was encountered by the group.

The opening days of November brought a new experience for some 56th pilots. Eight Thunderbolts from each squadron composed the group's contribution to escort B-24s bound for Gelsenkirchen on the 1st. While over Holland, Maj 'Bunny' Comstock spotted intermittent dark smoke trails several thousand feet higher than his squadron. Recognising an Me 262, he turned his squadron to meet the jet fighter as it dived towards the rear of the bomber formation. It was seen to shoot down a P-51 and continue diving towards the Liberators as other escorting P-51s and the 56th's P-47s tried to intercept.

Evidently seeing his pursuers, the Me 262 pilot turned to the left and away from the bombers as he continued the dive. At around 10,000 ft he made a 180-degree climbing turn to the right to speed away over the cloud undercast This was a mistake, for he allowed the diving P-47s and P-51s to cut him off and open fire. The jet attempted to evade with a climbing turn to the left, allowing Lt Walter Groce's flight to use the momentum of their dive to come up on the enemy. Groce's fire caused the left engine to burst into flames. His aircraft disabled and in a spin, the Me 262 pilot was seen to bail out. Six pilots in three groups claimed this jet, and its destruction was finally awarded as a shared victory between Lt Groce and a Mustang pilot from the 352nd FG.

The following day three Me 262s bounced a flight from the 61st FS which was part of an escort for B-24s bombing a target at Bielefeld. Two

For a frontline fighter group, the most demoralising events were pilots being killed in non-operational flying accidents. This was particularly so when the victim was an old stager like John Eaves, who was an original combat pilot in the 62nd FS. Promoted to captain after completing his first tour, he returned to the 56th FG in the autumn of 1944 for a second spell with the squadron. On 10 October, just a few days after his arrival at Boxted, he was leading a training flight in the Debden area when his P-47D (42-28812/LM-T) suffered engine failure. Eaves attempted a dead-stick landing in a field but the aircraft careered across a road, the far bank tearing off the engine and two trees smashing the wings. Eaves was crushed by the impact and died

P-47s suffered cannon shell damage from this surprise pass, and the 'blow-jobs' (as jets were popularly known by American pilots) kept on going, so there was no opportunity to engage in combat. Other Me 262s seen by 56th pilots that day easily out-distanced the Thunderbolts. The Messerschmitt jet fighter, along with the far rarer rocket-powered Me 163, had been encountered on other occasions by Eighth Air Force fighters, but this spate of engagements was the first time pilots from the 56th FG had been exposed to them. With a top speed some 100 mph greater than the P-47 and P-51, the jet had no problem in outrunning the opposition. However, the Jumo turbojet engines fitted to the Me 262 were still underdeveloped and boasted poor reliability. Should one of these fail in flight, then the speed superiority enjoyed by the Luftwaffe pilot in his heavy twin-engined fighter immediately vanished.

The threat of the Me 262 was met with identification of their bases and Allied patrols sent to pick off the jets when most vulnerable – during take-off and landing. Although the Me 262 had a formidable armament of four 30 mm cannon in the nose (and thus its pilot did not have the ranging problems inherent with wing-mounted weapons), the aircraft's high closing speed against its slower quarries dissipated effective strikes.

During strafing and bombing assaults on an oil storage facility at Langenselbold and the airfield at Schaafheim, in western Germany, on 18 November, enemy fighters intercepted were identified as both Bf 109 and Fw 190 types. Although two 56th pilots failed to return, the air battle again came out in favour of the group, with 11 aerial claims and 5 more enemy aircraft destroyed on the ground.

Once again this mission tally reflected the poor standard of Luftwaffe replacement pilots, and the superior training of their adversaries. With equally matched pilots, an Fw 190 should have been more than able to hold its own against a P-47D. The many variants of the Bf 109G family were less well matched, for this once excellent interceptor had been so weighed down with extra equipment that much of its performance advantage over the larger Thunderbolt had been lost. Pilot proficiency and tactics were frequently the deciding factor, particularly so in the 56th.

Undoubtedly the P-51 was a better fighter for the long-range escort mission, and the Eighth Air Force was steadily converting the last of its P-47 groups to the more nimble Mustang. However, the 56th's pride in its association and achievements with the Thunderbolt made it reluctant to part company. Nor did Republic Aviation, who saw the 56th as the standard bearer for its product, wish to see such separation.

Towards the end of 1944 word came to Boxted that a new, faster model P-47 would be available before long. If the Thunderbolts could not range as far as the Mustangs, at least their duration had been pushed up to over four hours. By fixing 108- or 150-US gallon tanks under each wing pylon, it was possible to haul a 500-lb GP bomb under the belly deep into western Germany. As always, the limiting factor was the amount of internal fuel available after auxiliary tanks had been released.

The chances of contact with the enemy were increased when in late November a MEW (Microwave Early Warning) station began operating from Gulpen, in the Netherlands, close to the German border. MEW was a radar technique similar to Type 16, but with better definition and longer range. It enabled controllers to vector fighters to hostile tracks up to 200 miles from the station. The 56th started using this new MEW station on 25 November.

Two days later MEW was used to direct Eighth Air Force fighters to several unsuspecting formations of enemy aircraft with the result that no fewer than 98 were claimed shot out of the sky. The 56th only manged to 'bag' four of these however, with Mustang groups taking the honours – extra duration played in favour of the P-51 once again. On 2 December the 'Wolfpack' was more fortunate, and while flying area support for a task force of B-24s, it was advised by MEW of hostile tracks heading for the bombers.

Following directions from a fighter controller, Maj Paul Conger led the 56th's P-47s down from 23,000 ft through cloud, emerging at 18,000 ft to see a *Gruppe*-strength enemy fighter formation some three miles ahead. Conger's squadron overhauled these Bf 109s for a successful bounce. A confused air battle ensued, and yet again the 56th could claim a decisive victory with 11 of the enemy downed. Three P-47s did not return – two were destroyed in a collision and their pilots killed, while the third was thought to have succumbed to vertigo in cloud.

COMBAT REPORT

MEW control was able to vector the 56th to a large formation of enemy fighters on 2 December 1944. The Group Leader, Maj Paul Conger, described what happened;

'Our mission was a fighter sweep ahead of the bombers, and we flew to the vicinity of Koblenz between two cloud layers at approximately 20,000 ft, before making a sweeping turn to the north, being in constant touch with MEW control, (call sign) Nuthouse.

'After ten minutes flying due north, Nuthouse reported bogies 30 to 40 miles still due north of us. I continued the vector at 20,000 ft, with a solid thin overcast 1000 ft below us.

'The next report from Nuthouse was: "Boggies are now south of you." I immediately made a 180-degree turn, but as yet we had seen nothing.

'Assuming that what Nuthouse was reporting must be below the overcast, I went through in a shallow dive. As we broke out I observed about 20 or more single-engined bogies flying about two or three miles ahead of us in a hostile type formation – tight line abreast, operating in sections of eight, each section close in line abreast but stacked down.

'As we closed we stayed quite well hidden in the overcast for nearly five minutes before we could identify them. Finally the gaggle became obviously Me 109s, carrying belly tanks. They still had not seen us, so I called the group to drop belly tanks. The fun was on.

'I closed to the middle of the formation as my squadron was nearing an offensive line abreast formation, too. I closed to 200 yards and throttled back indicating only 210 mph.

'Not having to span the Me 109 with the K-14 sight at all, I gave a two-second burst at what I assumed to be the lead ship. I immediately observed hits on the canopy and fuselage and the 109 was definitely out of control as it went off to the left. A second later, the pilot bailed out. His plane, still intact, spun downwards.

'The Jerry formation was still doing very little evasive action, so I skidded to the right and picked out another Me 109. I gave it a quick spurt at about 200 yards, observing plenty of hits in the canopy and coolant. Pieces were seen to fly off and the right side of the engine was on fire as the 109 went into a tight turn to the right. Two more small explosions occurred as the enemy aircraft went into an uncontrollable, inverted, flat spin.

'Unfortunately, as I was turning for other engagements, two Me 109s bounced me at 18,000 ft. I tried to turn right and climb, but after two turns they were out-climbing and out-turning me. I finally went straight down and was able to out-dive them as I hit the bottom cloud layer at 5000 ft.'

During the autumn and winter of 1944 the Eighth Air Force bombers, at great cost, made several attacks on the major synthetic oil plant at Leuna, near Meresburg. Considerable damage was wrought on most of these missions, but some vital installations were still able to function. It was suggested that a low-level attack by fighter-bombers could achieve what the 'heavies' had so far failed to do.

The plan called for Col Schilling to lead a force of 12 bomb-carrying P-47s, four from each unit. In view of the known defences, it appeared to be something of a suicide mission. Despite careful planning, and practise flights against a substitute target in England, the mission was never flown for the 'heavies' eventually reduced Leuna's oil production to a trickle.

Weather conditions in north-west Europe during autumn and winter 1944 were particularly adverse for flying, with one low after another bringing cloud and precipitation in from the Atlantic. Although Boxted is situated in the UK area with the lowest average annual rainfall (some 19 inches), it was often dampened with drizzle and draped with low cloud.

With fighter navigation then depending solely on dead reckoning and radio receipts, it is remarkable that so few pilots fell victim to the weather, the vast majority bringing their aircraft safely back to home base. But during the second week of December a still period of fog descended on England and the adjacent continental area of Europe, the like of which was not to be seen again in the 20th Century. At first a persistent overcast necessitating climbs of several thousand feet soon after take-off to escape from cloud, and on return, pilots often had to divert to other airfields because Boxted was 'socked in'.

Radio men check out the communication equipment fitted into Don Smith's *"OLE' COCK III"* on 9 November 1944. This aircraft was serviced by S/Sgt Safford's crew, who had previously looked after Gabreski's aircraft when it had been parked on the same hardstanding

COMBAT REPORT

The 23 December 1944 mission – the most successful in terms of aerial victories claimed by the 56th – produced numerous personal combat reports. The following account is the report lodged by 63rd FS CO, Maj Harold Comstock, who was an original combat pilot of the squadron then near the end of his second tour. His attacks were made with only the left guns firing, as those in the right wing had not been cocked by the armourer;

Personal Combat Report
VIII Air Force F.O.1445A
Major Harold E Comstock

a. Combat
b. 23 December 1944
c. 63rd Fighter Squadron, 56th Fighter Group
e. SW of Bonn
f. CAVU
g. FW 190s
h. Two FW 190s destroyed; 2 FW 190 damaged
I. A/C No 44-20455

I was leading Daily Squadron with a flight consisting of myself, F/O Hughes, Lts Schers and Clark. Nuthouse reported bandits in the area NW of Koblenz. We immediately found them. There were 60-plus FW 190s orbiting and climbing to the left. We came in from 25,000 ft above, with the sun at 4 o'clock to us. I made one pass through the middle of the formation of 190s and damaged one in the left wing. Pulling up, I turned head-on into the circle and one FW 190 turned out of the orbit to fire at me. We both started firing at 1000 yards. His shots were below and when I hit him in the engine he stopped firing altogether. He broke to the left and down. When I turned to follow him his engine was going very slow and as I pulled in behind him, he jettisoned his canopy and jumped. The FW went into a shallow diving turn.

I then pulled up and found myself underneath another FW 190 who could not see me. I stayed under him until he rolled out of the turn and then raised up right behind him. I opened fire at 200 yards, observing strikes all along the right side. Closing to 100 yards, there were more strikes on the right side with pieces flying off. I then observed another FW 190 on the deck, so I pulled in behind him and fired from about 50 yards, observing very few strikes on the fuselage before I was out of ammunition.

I claim two (2) FW 190s destroyed and two (2) FW 190s damaged.

Harold E Comstock
Major, Air Corps
Ammo fired: 1229 rds API

From 18 December the fog shroud came to ground level, and for four days operations were not tenable despite the urgent need for action, von Runstedt having launched his counter attack through the Ardennes that threatened the port of Antwerp. What followed was popularly known as the 'Battle of the Bulge'.

On the 23rd the fog lifted sufficiently to allow some 400 B-17s and B-24s to be despatched to strike communication lines behind the Ardennes area. The bombers were supported by the dozen Eighth Air Force fighter groups that could safely get airborne. The Luftwaffe was up in force to support the Wehrmacht offensive, and lost near 80 aircraft that day in air battles. The major contributor to that total was the 56th FG, whose pilots enjoyed their most succesful day of the war if enemy aircraft shot down was the yardstick by which this was measured.

To meet the urgency of the situation a maximum effort was flown, with 56 P-47Ds taking off from Boxted, led by the group CO. Mechanical and equipment turn-backs, which reduced strength on most missions, caused eight aircraft to return early. Once again under MEW control, the group was tasked to conduct a sweep in the Bonn and Coblenz areas.

More servicing activity at Boxted on 9 November 1944, this time centred around Mike Gladych's assigned P-47D 44-19718/HV-M. This aircraft had disruptive pattern camouflage in two shades of dark grey on the upper surfaces, light sky blue undersurfaces and red fuselage code letters. His 'scoreboard' featured 18 bold crosses for air victories and eight dull crosses for aircraft destroyed by strafing

Within 50 minutes of take-off, the group was being given vectors to large concentrations of hostile aircraft. The first, observed north of Bonn, disappeared among the clouds, although another large hostile formation was then seen to the south, causing Schilling to question MEW control as to why they had not been vectored to these tracks. The response was to hold to the vector given, and shortly thereafter two enemy formations of an estimated 40-plus Bf 109s and 60-plus Fw 190s were seen. The squadrons of the 56th flying between 23,500 and 25,000 ft had between a 1000- and 2000-ft height advantage.

Schilling directed his squadron (the 62nd FS) to spread out so that they might be mistaken for a Luftwaffe formation joining up, for their approach was being made from the rear. This ruse worked, with the enemy unaware of what was happening until the Thunderbolts opened fire. In the course of the next few minutes Col Schilling personally shot down five enemy aircraft, while the remaining members of his squadron claimed a total of 14. The fight was not all one-sided, for two P-47s were also shot down.

Maj Comstock, leading the 63rd FS, tackled the Fw 190s, which were thought to include some 'long-nosed' Fw 190Ds amongst their ranks. The 63rd pilots claimed 13 of the enemy and the 61st FS, providing top cover, five. One 63rd P-47 went down during the mêlée, whilst another with serious battle damage managed to regain Allied-held territory before the pilot had to bail out.

Returning to Boxted, total claims of 37 destroyed, one probably destroyed and 16 damaged were put in, but higher authority reassessed the evidence from gun camera film to reduce the former figure to 32. Even so, the group's total credits for air and ground destruction of enemy aircraft passed the 800-mark. Schilling, who received a Distinguished Service Cross award (his second) for his leadership of the 23 December mission, also then rated the leading Eighth Air Force fighter ace in combined air and ground victories.

MEW control helped the 56th to 16 more victory claims before the New Year, despite inclement weather with freezing fog which led into a period of snow and ice. For the groundcrews this was probably their most trying time since arrival in England.

P-47Ms AND LUFTWAFFE JETS

Early in January 1945, the 78th FG completed its conversion from P-47s to P-51s, which left the 56th FG as the last of the Eighth Air Force's 15 fighter groups still flying Thunderbolts. The first of the new P-47M models arrived at Boxted on 3 January, and this was immediately earmarked for Col Schilling's use. Externally, the P-47M appeared little different from a late D-model, for the aircraft was basically only a P-47D fitted with a revised version of the R-2800 – the C model, which had been developed for the US Navy to power carrier-borne fighters.

All 108 production model P-47Ms – the fastest propeller-driven aircraft to see operational service with the Allies – were destined for the 56th FG. Even at this late stage in the war, the group still expected to be moved to a continental airfield, so camouflage was applied to the upper surfaces of the newly-delivered fighters. However, this took the form more of a distinctive decoration than camouflage, and was yet another example of the group flaunting its élite status as the leading fighter group in Europe.

All 61st FS P-47Ms were to have matt black upper surfaces with red identification letters and tail numbers, while 62nd FS aircraft would sport a grey and green disruptive pattern with yellow letters and numbers, and the 63rd's Thunderbolts displayed a disruptive pattern in two shades of blue, with 'silver' letters and blue tail numbers.

The first use of the P-47M on operations came on 14 January when Paul Conger flew one to claim a Bf 109 (taking his tally to 9.5 aerial kills)

The 56th's second anniversary of arrival in England was an occasion for a party on 6 January 1945, the cooks having made a giant cake for all to sample. Seven senior officers – the last of the original combat pilots still with the group – posed for the camera, but Paul Conger, who was on the end of the line, doesn't appear in this picture. Seen left to right are Jim Carter, Don Smith, 'Bunny' Comstock, Dave Schilling, Pete Dade and Les Smith. There individual aerial victory credits were 6, 5.5, 5, 22.5, 3 and 7. Conger had 8.5 at this time, but would subsequently add another three before ending his tour

whilst leading the group into another successful combat. A very large formation of Fw 190s, with Bf 109 top cover, had been engaged near Magdeburg, and aside from Conger's kill, a further ten aircraft were claimed for the loss of one P-47 and its pilot. A second pilot lost his life when engine failure forced him to bail out over the sea. ASR was on the scene within 15 minutes, but the pilot had already succumbed to the extreme cold. It was estimated that an airman would die of exposure after three minutes' immersion in the North Sea during winter.

P-47Ms had arrived in sufficient numbers by mid January for the 61st FS to shed its Ds and re-equip with the new model. Unfortunately, enthusiasm for the M began to wane when several pilots reported misfiring and an inability to extract full power at high altitude. Then, on 21 January, a 61st P-47M suffered complete engine failure while at 32,000 ft in the vicinity of the base. Its pilot, 2Lt Ed Lightfoot, skilfully maintained control in a gliding descent to belly the aircraft in at Boxted. Inspection revealed cracks in the ignition high tension leads, and these were also found on other P-47Ms. Similar trouble had been experienced with P-47Cs when the group first came to England, and leads with more durable insulation had to be fitted.

It appears that when installing the 'C' model engine, supplying toughened leads had been overlooked. Replacing the ignition harness on all M-models took some time, and it meant that 61st FS pilots had to revert to flying the D-models still employed by the remaining two squadrons within the 56th. The lack of power at high altitude was a different problem entirely, and was found to be caused by the correlation of throttle and turbo-supercharges settings – another problem that had been encountered with the P-47C.

Dave Schilling had now completed well over 400 hours operational flying, and was ordered to hand over command of the 56th and take a desk post at the controlling fighter wing headquarters. On 27 January he left for Saffron Walden and the 65th FW, 'Pete' Dade inheriting command of the 56th. Les Smith became his deputy and Felix Williamson took Smith's place as leader of the 62nd FS. A week earlier Paul Conger had assumed command of the 63rd FS when Harold Comstock completed his second tour and left for the USA.

Snow and freezing conditions contributed to several crash-landings during January 1945. D-model Thunderbolt 42-26986/LM-I *Lil Miss Wolf* careered off the end of runway 34, skidded across a public road and lost its tail

Winging back over the cold North Sea, P-47D 42-28824/UN-A had previously served with another group that had converted to Mustangs. Several other replacement aircraft received by the 56th in the latter part of 1944 had also seen service elsewhere

It was Conger who on 3 February led the longest-duration mission ever undertaken by the group, some – five-and-a-half-hours. Tasked to carry out a sweep of the Berlin area ahead of the bombers heading for targets around that city, the P-47 pilots gradually climbed out over liberated areas of the continent to conserve fuel and oxygen. Clear skies prevailed from England to Berlin, where a formation of Fw 190s seen some distance below was successfully attacked. Eight were claimed destroyed for the loss of one P-47 and its pilot. It was a well needed fillip for group morale.

While two 150-US gallon drop tanks could be carried under the wings of the P-47, the drag they created was considerable. The shackle pylons on the wings also caused drag, affecting both manoeuvrability and speed. Dave Schilling had discussed these problems with Cas Hough, who was in charge of the experiment station at Bovingdon, and the latter's solution was the 215-US gallon belly tank. Basically a wider version of the 'flat' 150-gallon tank, it was fabricated in steel by a British firm specially for the 56th FG. Use of this tank allowed the wing pylons to be removed, thus further maximising the Thunderbolt's performance.

P-47Ms had begun to be assigned to the 62nd FS in early February, followed later in the month by the first aircraft for the 63rd. However, engine failures still continued to plague the M-model, with a 62nd pilot being killed in one on 3 February, whilst on the 9th a 61st pilot managed to survive collision with two small oaks when forced to crash-land in a field near the base. Even so, the 61st FS became operational with the M on St Valentine's Day, but pilots from the unit experienced no immediate love affair with these aircraft.

Technical problems that plagued the aircraft on this and following missions eventually led to a grounding of all P-47Ms on the station later in the month. Defective carburettor diaphragms and engine cylinder over-cooling were the next problems identified, although the most worrying discovery of them all was the corrosion found in the cylinder bores of an engine recovered from a crashed aircraft.

Similar corrosion was found in other 'C' engines, and it was deduced that they had lacked insufficient protection from the elements during shipment from the USA. A programme of engine changing was begun that eventually involved three-quarters of all the P-47Ms at Boxted! While so many aircraft were grounded, mission strengths were much reduced, with only the retained D-models of the 62nd and 63rd in use. This created a nightmare situation for the engineering officers, with a combined total of 140 D- and M-models on the station, plus a dozen war-weary P-51Bs which were brought in to give the pilots conversion training in case the problems with the new Thunderbolt could not be cured.

By the middle of March all three squadrons were able to put up whole formations of P-47Ms, and by 24 March, when the Allies launched Operation *Varsity* and crossed the Rhine, the remaining P-47Ds and the P-51s had gone.

Air combats were now rare, for with the Luftwaffe's fast declining activity it was not only a case of being in the right place at the right time, as it had always been in successful air fighting, but that Allied fighters were now so numerous over the shrinking Third Reich that competition for aerial kills was overwhelming. The P-47Ms flown by Lts Ball, Lear and Gould put paid to two rare Arado Ar 234 jet bombers caught flying low on 14 March. Eleven days later Maj George Bostwick (who had recently been given command of the 63rd) and 2Lt Edwin Crosthwait of the same squadron each claimed an Me 262 as the jets orbited the airfield at Parchim.

In early April there were more interceptions of Me 262s, although the jet pilots usually used their superior speed to escape. On 5 April Capt John

Maj Paul Conger's groundcrew attended to *Bernyce,* P-47M 44-21134/UN-P. The 63rd FS ace made the first operational use of the P-47M when he led the 56th FG on the 14 January 1945 Rodeo in this aircraft. He was credited with shooting down a Bf 109 and damaging a second Messerschmitt fighter during the course of this mission

COMBAT REPORT

An MEW-controlled sweep over western Germany on 25 February 1945 brought no contact with enemy aircraft, so the group went down to look for communication targets to shoot up. An attack on a freight train brought an unexpected result, as 1Lt Charles McBath reported;

'We were strafing road and rail transportation in the vicinity north of Schweinfurt when, at a split in the railroad tracks at 5010N-1004E, Capt Flagg and I went down to strafe some 15 or more boxcars standing on a siding.

'While strafing the cars length-wise, the whole train suddenly exploded in front of me, with flames shooting way up, and smoke belching from the explosion. As I was so close I had no other alternative but to fly right through the base of the explosion, which immediately engulfed me in complete darkness, punctuated only by large spurts of flame, completely covering my plane. Then I felt as if I had flown into the train because the plane reacted similarly to one that is being bellied in, and the inside of the cockpit seemed to be on fire. Coming out of the smoke, a quick backward glance revealed a dense cumulus cloud reaching some 5000 ft, with flames up to 1000 ft.

'I also noticed that my airplane was severely damaged, so I readied myself to bail out. The right side of the engine was spouting oil in a heavy stream, and the engine itself was smoking badly. Approximately one foot was blown off the left stabiliser and it partly jammed the elevator actions. Both wings had numerous holes in them, my right wing being partly on fire, and the right side of the canopy completely blown off. To add to my troubles the prop was set at 1800 RPMs and I was unable to change the pitch.

'Being over enemy territory, I gave a second thought to bailing out, and then decided to see if I could keep going and maybe make it safely to a point behind our lines.

'I started due west, attempting to avoid an intense barrage of flak at about 3000 ft. Shortly thereafter, my flight leader, Capt Walter Flagg, called me on the R/T and guided me safely around a heavy barrage of rocket flak through which I would have otherwise flown through, had he not been there.

'Again I contemplated bailing out. Smoke and oil from the engine had filled the cockpit, and the plane was liable to explode at any second.

'I called in, asking how long it would take to get to friendly territory, and was told by Fairbanks that it would be about 20 minutes. With this in mind, I stayed with the ship, but after 30 minutes I was still fairly deep in Germany.

'The smoke was heavier and, by now, the oil had covered the entire fuselage. The cockpit was so badly flooded with oil that I couldn't see my instruments. My hands and feet kept sliding off the controls. The elevators were jammed to about five or ten degrees play, and I could sense the stick jam when I tried to climb.

'Throughout the entire flight back Capt Flagg stayed with me, offering me protection from any possible enemy attack, giving me courage, advice and confidence without which I am sure I could never have gone that far.

'About 35 miles from the front lines, Capt Flagg "talked me in" to a field, where I made a blind and wheels down landing. Landing, my plane ran off the runway, and I jumped out while a fire crew sprang up immediately to put out the small fires in my smoking engine.

'To this day I will never know or understand how my aircraft flew from the scene of the explosion to A-82 (Verdun), but thanks to a P-47, and even more so Captain Flagg's intrepid nature, guidance and judgement, I was able to get back to friendly territory.'

McBath was awarded a well deserved DFC for his conduct on this mission.

Fahringer shot down one caught in a turn, and two days later George Bostwick damaged another, as well as putting paid to two Bf 109s that went for the bombers under escort. Three other 63rd FS pilots also claimed Bf 109s this day.

In an effort to locate increasingly elusive enemy aircraft, an airborne radar was installed in a two-seat conversion of a war-weary P-47D, and on 9 April Col Dade flew the former fighter at the head of a free-lance mis-

Walter Sharbo shot down an Me 262 on 10 April 1945, and this proved to be the last enemy aircraft to fall to the guns of a 62nd FS Thunderbolt

sion to the Regensburg area. The equipment didn't function and the Luftwaffe was not seen.

The next day, when returning from a fighter sweep in the Berlin area, the 62nd FS spotted Me 262s. Lt Walter Sharbo shot one down and Capt Bill Wilkerson claimed another. These proved to be the last two enemy fighters to fall to the guns of the 56th FG in air combat. They were also the only aerial claims on a day when Eighth Air Force fighters shot up several airfields in Germany, and were credited with destroying 309 aircraft and damaging another 237 on the ground. The 56th was responsible for 45.5 of the destroyed total (and 53 damaged) by strafing at four airfields. The ground fire encountered caused damage of varying degrees to 15 P-47s, one apparently crashing and killing its pilot while attempting to land at a continental airfield.

Another free-lance mission on 13 April turned into the most successful day's airfield strafing ever for the group. Detailed to patrol the German-Danish peninsula, and with permission to strafe, pilots were presented with a study of Luftwaffe bases in the area at their briefing. In the early afternoon 48 P-47Ms (plus three spares) set out from Boxted, making landfall near Hamburg 70 minutes later. On the way two pilots had to abort the mission with technical problems, one of whom was 61st FS CO, Jim Carter.

Flying on to Denmark, the group overflew Eggebeck airfield and found it lined with aircraft – an estimated 150-plus of several types. Lt Col 'Pete' Dade, leading the 63rd FS, took two flights down to attack any flak posi-

tions, leaving the rest of his squadron at 10,000 ft and the other two units circling at 5000 and 10,000 ft above that height. The first passes across the airfield brought no ground fire, so the rest of the 63rd were called down to strafe. It was only then that the airfield defences opened up, and one P-47 apparently took crippling hits in the engine.

Lt William Hoffman gained some altitude before bailing out, but he was still too low and his parachute did not have time to open fully. He was the last 56th FG pilot to be killed in action. Despite his loss, ground fire was considered weak, and when the 63rd had expended most of its ammunition, the 62nd and 61st, in turn, came down to shoot at the many aircraft to be seen. The group returned home to Boxted with claims of 95 destroyed and 95 damaged pushing its overall tally of combined air and ground victories past the 1000 destroyed mark. Many pilots scored multiple victories on this mission, but 1Lt Randell Murphy beat them all when his combat film showed him shooting up ten enemy aircraft that subsequently rated destroyed credits.

Fittingly, the attack on Eggebeck airfield took place on the date that the 56th celebrated the second anniversary of its first group combat mission.

A further strafing venture on 16 April resulted in the 56th's last ground claims for enemy aircraft, four being destroyed and five damaged at heavily defended locations. Capt Edward Appel's P-47 was hit and crashed on a nearby hill, although the pilot extricated himself safely and evading capture. This was the last of 128 Thunderbolts that the group was to have posted missing in action. Mustang groups claimed over 700 strafing vic-

This 62nd FS formation of P-47Ms shows off the individual camouflage patterns of green and grey. Note that the leading edges of the wings and tailplane remained unpainted. The aircraft are flying over Boxted village, with the lead P-47M being Lt Sharbo's 44-21214/LM-Y

tories on this day but at the cost of 30 of their number. After further high losses on the 17th, strafing was generally forbidden.

The great strafing forays by Eighth Air Force fighters in the closing days of hostilities saw other groups produce equally high claims. The 56th was more fortunate than some of the Mustang units, which suffered such high losses in this dangerous activity that some senior officers queried whether such attacks were necessary, for it was suspected that the Luftwaffe had no fuel to fly most of the aircraft on its airfields. But there was always the possibility of one last great show of force, and for this reason alone these strafing missions were justified.

The two-seat 'Doublebolt' was tried again on the 17 April bomber escort mission but no enemy tracks were detected. Missions on the 18th, 20th and 21st were equally barren. The mission of the 21st was to be the last of 447 (464 if including separations for different duties) flown by the group, although this was unknown at the time. A and B formations were

Lt Donald Armstrong stands alongside his P-47M 44-21230/LM-A. The code letters had only been marked out on the camouflage and had yet to be painted in insignia yellow when this photograph was taken

Fin fillets to give 'bubble' canopy Thunderbolts better lateral stability were installed 'in the field' on P-47Ms at Boxted in the early spring of 1945. This unpainted example, seen on P-47M 44-21131/UN-X, was a late addition. The officer peering behind the intercooler door is believed to be 1Lt Robert Bailey, who was the pilot assigned to this aircraft

despatched, with the former (led by Felix Williamson) on bomber support to Salzburg and the latter (headed by by Joe Perry), with 18 P-47s, a free-lance to Munich. The B-24s were recalled when extensive cloud prevented visual bombing, so the A force also went on a free-lance sweep. The only other aircraft seen were Allied.

COMBAT REPORT

Lt Col Lucian A Dade's report of the 56th's strafing marathon at Eggebeck is recounted in full;

'On April 13, 1945 the Group was ordered to give free-lance support in the target area including the German-Danish peninsula, Hamburg, Berlin and north-west to the Baltic. The Group made landfall north of Hamburg and swept north to Eggebeck air-drome as briefed, at 1510 hours. The squadrons then took position, with 62nd top cover at 15,000 ft, 61st at 10,000 ft and Blue Section of the 63rd with eight ships orbiting the field in string at 5000 ft, and were to roll down and strafe any gun position that might open fire on either White or Red Flights.

'I was leading the White Section of the 63rd with eight ships, and briefed these ships to make the ini-tial flak run from south to north in an attempt to silence the known positions. The first pass was initi-ated from 9000 ft and hit the deck approximately three miles south of the field. Both flights were line abreast and indicating between 400 and 450 mph. Three flak positions were identified and sprayed but none seemed to be manned. Both flights continued on the deck to a point about two miles north of the airdrome before recovering, White Flight to the left and Red Flight to the right. I received a hit by 20 mm from a small village about three miles north-west of the airdrome and also a .30 calibre that seemed to be explosive. This gun position was not strafed as it could easily be avoided.

'There were an estimated 150 to 200 aircraft of all descriptions on the airdrome and on two satellite fields, one to the north and one to the south. White and Red Flights of the 63rd again made passes from the south, concentrating on the south-west and north-west dispersal. After this pass no serious flak was encountered, both Blue and Yellow Flights being called down to strafe.

'After five passes it was necessary for me to abort due to oil on windshield and canopy. At this time only the 63rd Squadron was strafing, and I counted 14 aircraft destroyed. Seven were in the south-west dispersal, five in the north-west dispersal and five along the hangar line.

'In all, this squadron made 140 individual passes, firing 31,148 rounds on the south-west, north-west and hangar line and area north of the field adjacent to the railroad. The area was so covered by smoke drifting from west to east that it was impossible to count individual fires. However, the two squadrons orbiting above estimated 40 to 50 as the 63rd left the airdrome.

'The next squadron down was the 61st, and their passes were made as follows: from south-east to north-west in the dispersal at the south-west corner. They then concentrated their passes on the north-west and northern area. Most of their passes were made on these two areas from south to north. This squadron made 94 individual passes, firing 22,243 rounds. Their claims were 25 destroyed.

'The 62nd Squadron was then called down to strafe. At this point Lt Colonel Renwick, leading the 62nd, made the following estimates: fifteen-plus fires in the southern area, thirty-plus in the north-west and hangar area and ten-plus in the north-west section. This squadron made its first passes from north-west to south-east on the revetment area north-west of the field, then concentrated one flight on the area adjacent to the railroad just to the north-east of the field, while another flight, Blue, made passes on the area north of the airdrome coming in from north to south. At the same time Yellow Flight was clearing the remainder of the north-west area and two planes on the field, one being on the north-west/south-east runway. The squadron made a total of 105 passes expending 24,682 rounds and claim-ing 26 destroyed.

'The total for the Group being 339 individual passes and expending 78,073 rounds. I feel that the 95 aircraft claimed destroyed are completely justifi-able, and with such evidence as combat film, K-25 pictures and supporting statements from individual pilots, this figure is to be found accurate.'

FINAL DAYS IN ENGLAND

The end of hostilities in Europe was officially declared as 8 May 1945, following which the 56th FG expected to be moved to Germany for occupational duties. Just as it had expected to be moved to a base in liberated France or Belgium following the successful Allied land campaign of the previous summer, this posting was also never realised, and the group remained at Boxted for another four months.

After the final round of missions, the 56th's score of enemy aircraft destroyed stood at 1005.5, whilst its great rival the 4th FG had claimed 1002. These figures were to be frequently revised during the next few weeks as information was received from Germany and from airmen returned from captivity. VIII Fighter Command issued its final tallies on for its fighter groups in September, the 4th having its score elevated to 1052.5 whilst the 56th's was reduced to 985.5. These changes largely resulted from the inspection of airfields strafed in the final weeks of war.

P-47M 44-21228/LM-K cavorts over the patchwork of rural Suffolk in spring sunshine. Two smoke and chemical dispensing tanks are carried on the wing shackles. These were never used operationally by the group

However, when it came to aerial combat victories the 56th was far and away the leader with 674.5, followed by the 357th FG with 609.5. In later years a further re-assessment boosted the 56th's score to 677 and reduced the 357th's to 575. giving the 'Wolfpack' a clear 100-plus lead over any other fighter group in the ETO. This numbers game had been fostered by high command as a morale builder, for they believed it developed a competitive spirit among the fighter groups – it was the leadership of the 56th that had started this particular ball rolling.

Eighth Air Force high command also gave its blessing to aircraft destroyed by strafing being equal to those shot down, this reward acknowledging that attacking airfields was a far more dangerous business than air-to-air fighting, particularly in the last six to eight months of the war. In post-war years, USAF historians perceived no more credit due to fighter pilots attacking parked aircraft than those shooting up other ground targets where heavy defensive fire were encountered.

The precise number of aircraft shot down by an individual pilot is in most cases forever in doubt. An apparently disintegrating enemy aircraft in a gun camera film has been known to have survived. Alternatively, one assessed as only damaged has been found to have been destroyed. An individual's total claims can be either more or less than the true figure, and the same applies to group scores. Nevertheless, the margin of lead in the recorded figures indicates that the 56th was the most successful group in air combat.

P-47M 44-21175, which was originally coded UN-D, had its decor removed in June 1945 and was then painted up to represent 'Hub' Zemke's UN-Z, complete with artwork that flamboyantly praised the group's wartime achievements. This aircraft had been decorated by the 56th following a request from the Eighth Air Force for a P-47 for display at the victory exposition held under the Eiffel Tower in Paris. The aircraft is seen outside No 1 hangar at Boxted, shortly before being flown to France

Moreover, the larger share of its victories were obtained when the Luft-waffe still had a fighter force to be reckoned with – before the attrition wrought during the winter of 1943 and following spring had resulted in the haemorrhaging of skilled pilots that could not be replaced. The 56th also had the best overall losses-to-claims ratio of near eight per cent for combined air and ground, and over five per cent for air alone.

Of the 128 P-47s posted missing in action, nearly two-thirds were lost in ground attack. Of the pilots, 36 survived as prisoners of war, eight evaded capture and 84 were killed. But the enemy was not alone in taking life, for another 48 pilots were lost in flying accidents – a not untypical total for a fighter group at a time when flying was a dangerous business. Eighteen of these occurred before leaving the US in 1942 and two in Eng-land following the end of combat. Twenty-seven pilots were wounded, two twice. Eighteen 56th FG pilots received their nation's second highest award for bravery, the Distinguished Service Cross, and one pilot, David Schilling, won a DSC Oak Leaf Cluster. There were 28 awards of the third-ranking decoration, the Silver Star.

The total operational flying hours in the 447 missions amounted to 64,302 for 19,391 sorties. Bomb tonnage delivered ran to 678 short tons, while 59 air-to-ground rocket projectiles were fired. Ammunition expended amounted to 3,063,345 rounds of 0.50 calibre.

By VE-Day only three of the original pilot complement that came to England in December 1942 remained with the group – Col Lucien Dade, the CO, Lt Col Donald Renwick, the Deputy CO, and Maj James Carter, the Group Operations Officer. These three officers remained at Boxted for some weeks, but many of the long-serving groundcrewmen were soon on their way home.

A points system, based on service time and deployment, was devised by high command to determine individuals' priorities for return to the USA. Personnel replacements were recent arrivals in Europe, or those with low points totals. Many had to be trained for duties with a fighter group – in particular specialist engineering or maintenance. A training programme was instigated, but proved difficult to pursue with the constant personnel changes, although P-47Ms were flown on training missions until late August, with air-to-air firing at towed drogues and air-to-ground on ranges in the Wash and elsewhere.

There were many detachments for pilots, with some even going on exchange with the RAF, where one lost his life in a Typhoon. One of those to temporarily detached was Capt Fred McIntosh of the 62nd FS, who received orders to join a special flight that was ferrying selected Luftwaffe types from Germany to an airfield near Cherbourg. These were then craned onto a Royal Navy aircraft carrier at Cherbourg and shipped to the USA for exploratory work at Wright Field. McIntosh's CO, Felix Williamson, and Deputy Group CO, Jim Carter, thought this an inter-esting appointment and managed to get themselves unofficially attached to its as well.

When the ferrying project was completed in late June there was appar-ently insufficient stowage for some of the types collected, and these remained on the airfield at Cherbourg – among them was a Heinkel He 111. Requiring transportation back to Boxted, the three 56th FG pilots hit on the idea of using this discarded aircraft. In the lax atmosphere

On 1 August 1945 Boxted was opened to the British public for US Army Air Forces Day, and many locals came to get a close-up view of the aircraft that had been a regular sight in the sky for the past 17 months. Small boys were allowed in the cockpit of this P-47M parked outside No 1 hangar. The author was one of them, if not so small

of the immediate post-war period, nobody was particularly concerned about the disposition of unwanted enemy aircraft, and on 2 July the appropriated Heinkel arrived at Boxted. An Fw 190 was to follow from the same source.

The Heinkel was duly painted up in 61st FS colours and was often to be seen in the East Anglian sky belching black smoke from the exhausts of its protesting engines. Unfortunately, the engine of the Fw 190 proved to be in such a poor state that the aircraft was considered unsafe for further flight and was eventually broken up.

One or two communication aircraft were also operated by the group during the operational period, including a retired B-26C Marauder. In May 1945 the 56th acquired its own war-weary B-17G which was converted for transport use.

In the weeks after VE-Day, the group was asked to prepare a P-47M for the USAAF exposition to be staged under the Eiffel Tower in Paris during July. The aircraft prepared was painted up to acknowledge the group's famous commander, 'Hub' Zemke, and it proudly carried the slogan *Zemke's Wolpack*.

In August Pete Dade left Boxted and Don Renwick became the 56th's last commander while in England. Early in September notice was given that the group would soon be on its way home, and that the various transfers and disposal of remaining equipment and stores should be effected. There remained the problem of the He 111, for which official sanction and documentation was lacking. This could not be unloaded on any other

USAAF establishment without the essential papers, and any attempt to do so might bring trouble for the individuals involved in appropriating the aircraft in the first place. Maj Carter threfore decided upon a little sub-terfuge.

Early one morning he flew the Heinkel to RAF North Weald, where he landed, parked and was then quickly picked up by another pilot flying the 56th's Marauder and returned to Boxted. Nothing was said to the RAF, who obviously assumed that the visitor would be collected. After a few days, when the RAF realised that the Heinkel had been abandoned, Carter and company were long gone.

Captured enemy aircraft were exhibited at Farnborough that autumn, and as no other flyable He 111 was available in the UK, this one was used. Later, put in storage, it eventually found its way to the RAF Museum at Hendon so that, ironically, the only aircraft extant that flew with the 56th FG is a former enemy aircraft.

On 9 September 1945 the group was officially transferred to Little Walden, an airfield close to the 65th FW Headquarters. However, the last formation of Thunderbolts did not leave Boxted until around 11 am on 14 September, bound for Speke. Here, the aircraft languished until bro-ken up. The remainder of the personnel withdrew next day, and Boxted was returned to the RAF. One body of ground personnel sailed for home in the *Europa* four days later, and the residue of the group at Little Walden boarded the *Queen Mary* on 11 October, reaching New York on the 16th. On arrival the party moved to Camp Kilmer and there, two days later, the 56th FG was inactivated.

As is the way with military organisations, the numerical designation would be given to new formations in the USAAF (and the independent United States Air Force that replaced the former organisation in Septem-ber 1947), but on 18 October 1945 the entity that was the 56th Fighter Group of World War 2 ceased to exist.

In air fighting the 56th was the most successful United States fighter group operating in the European Theatre of Operations. It was also responsible for several of the innovations that were adopted by other fighter organisations, but above all, through its determined leadership, competitive spirit and the general high quality of the pilots, it inspired other America fighter units, and led the way in besting the Luftwaffe. It was indeed an élite formation.

'Out to grass'. P-47M 44-21202/HV-P waits to be flown to the breakers in late August 1945. Code letters can just be discerned under the wing of *Joy Boy*. From mid-May 1945 code letters, black on metal, were carried under the left wings of all 56th FG Thunderbolts

APPENDICES

COLOUR PLATES

1

P-40F 41-13761 of Lt Eugene O'Neill, 62nd FS, Bendix Airport, New Jersey, April 1942

After making do with various types of fighter aircraft (most of which were obsolescent), the 56th FG received a sufficient number of newly-built P-40Fs in April 1942 to equip all three of its squadrons. The Curtiss fighters only remained in service with the group for a few months however, for in June the 56th started to receive P-47Bs. 41-13761 has a yellow-painted propeller spinner and forward fuselage to denote its assignment to the 62nd FS at Bendix Airport, New Jersey. The fighter was usually flown by Lt Eugene O'Neill during this period.

2

P-47B 41-6002 of Col Hubert Zemke, CO of the 56th FG, Bridgeport Municipal Airport, Connecticut, September 1942

Received by the 56th FG at Bridgeport Municipal Airport on 21 August 1942, 41-6002 was used by Col Zemke and painted up as the group commander's aircraft. This involved the division of the nose cowling band into the three squadron colours, plus encircling bands on the rear fuselage in these shades of red, yellow and blue for the 61st, 62nd and 63rd FSs, respectively. This aircraft was damaged in an accident on 10 October 1942, and after repair went to Westover Field on 20 November. It was finally written off in an accident on 14 January 1943.

3

P-47B 41-5999 of the 61st FS, Bridgeport Municipal Airport, Connecticut, September 1942

The P-47Bs used by the 56th FG during the second half of 1942 were frequently returned to the Republic plant for modifications, and most only remained in a squadron assignment for a few weeks. P-47B 41-5999 was delivered to the 61st FS at Bridgeport on 21 August 1942, the unit making use of 'plane-in-squadron' numbers in the 20s and 30s ranges for identification purposes. This Thunderbolt was destroyed in a fatal crash on 25 October 1942.

4

P-47C-5 41-6352 of Capt Donald Renwick, 61st FS, King's Cliffe, March 1943

When the 61st FS received its first P-47Cs at King's Cliffe, a system of 'plane-in-squadron' numbering similar to that used in the USA was considered, and some aircraft had crudely-painted two-digit numbers applied on their fuselage in Neutral Gray. This form of individual aircraft identification was soon abandoned in favour of a three-digit numbering system, but this too quickly gave way to the standard code letters eventually common to all RAF and USAAF day fighters in the ETO. P-47C 41-6352 became HV-T, and carried the name *Doc* in yellow on the engine cowling. Renwick claimed his only aerial victory in this

Thunderbolt on 17 August 1943, and flew most of his missions in 41-6352 until it was retired in January 1944.

5

P-47C-2 41-6322/"*LITTLE BUTCH*" of Capt Robert Wetherbee, 61st FS, Horsham St Faith, May 1943

Capt Robert Wetherbee, 61st FS A Flight commander, was shot down near Forges in *"LITTLE BUTCH"* on 26 June 1943. Four other 56th Thunderbolts and three pilots were lost this day, and two more badly mauled, when bounced by Fw 190s of JG 2. Interestingly, the aircraft name of the squadron CO, Maj Loren McCollom, was *Butch*.

6

P-47C-5 41-6330/"*MOY TAVARISH*" of Col Hubert Zemke, CO of the 56th FG, Horsham St Faith, June 1943

The personal aircraft of Col Hub Zemke, and flown by him on most of his early missions, this Thunderbolt bore the legend *"MOY TAVARISH"* ("My Comrade") for a few weeks in the spring of 1943. This reflected Zemke's time in the USSR with an RAF party during 1941. The big fighter also carried the ID letter code 'Z', which reflected the surname of the pilot, and was a privilege of rank afforded to flight, squadron and group commanders only. The name, victory symbols and spoked wheel motif seen in this profile were removed during the summer of 1943, as the colonel felt uneasy about the CO displaying such individualism. On 21 September 1943 Zemke had this aircraft moved from the 62nd to the 63rd FS for maintenance in furtherance of his wish not to be seen as favouring one squadron. Three of Zemke's credited victories were obtained with this aircraft, which was coded UN-S when in the 63rd. It was struck from the squadron's records after Lt Adam Wisniewski bellied the aircraft in at Manston on Christmas Eve 1943.

7

P-47C-2 41-6224/*TWO ROLL CHARLIE* of Lt Conway Saux, 62nd FS, Halesworth, June 1943

TWO ROLL CHARLIE was assigned to Lt Conway Saux. On 22 August 1943 Saux set off from Halesworth on a training mission in poor weather and was involved in a collision with P-47C 41-6189/LM-P, flown by Lt Don Tettemer. Saux bailed out but there was not enough height for his parachute to open and he was killed – the aircraft came down at Valley Farm, Henham. Tettemer died in the wreckage of his P-47, which fell at Sotherton.

8

P-47C-2 41-6203/*WINDY* of Lt Jack Brown, 63rd FS, Halesworth, June 1943

Received by the 63rd FS on 27 February 1943, 41-6203 was eventually assigned to Lt Jack Brown, who named it *WINDY* and later *The Flying Ute*. The fighter remained in service until 16 September 1943, when it was transferred to the 495th FTG at Atcham. As far as can be traced, no victories were obtained by any of the dozen pilots who flew this aircraft operationally. The yellow surround to the fuselage National Insignia was recommended by the British Air Ministry when P-47s prepared to become operational under RAF guidance.

9

P-47C 41-6584/*HOLY JOE* of Lt Joe Egan, 63rd FS, Halesworth, August 1943

Seen in standard P-47 camouflage and early ETO markings, this aircraft was used by five-victory ace Lt Joe Egan to down his first kill (an Fw 190) on 19 August 1943. This was the second C-model assigned to Egan, the first having been written off after a crash landing in May 1943. His remaining kills were scored in P-47D-10 42-75069/UN-E and P-47D-15 42-75855/UN-E. *Holy Joe* ended its service with the 56th in a crash-landing on 1 December 1943.

10

P-47C-2 41-6211/*JACKIE* of Capt Robert Lamb, 61st FS, Halesworth, August 1943

Like Joe Egan, future seven-kill ace Capt Robert Lamb used this aircraft to claim his first victory on 19 August (again an Fw 190). He was still flying it in mid-October, when he claimed an 'Me 210' damaged on the 18th. *Jackie* failed to return from the 1 December 1943 mission whilst being flown by Lt Jack Brown.

11

P-47D-2 42-22481/*Kentucky PUD II* of Lt Ralph Johnson, 62nd FS, Halesworth, August 1943

Assigned to Lt Ralph Johnson, 42-22481 was one of the first P-47s from the Evansville production plant to reach the 56th. Named *Kentucky Pud II*, it was used by Johnson to claim all three of his aerial victories. Retired from the frontline in early spring 1944, 42-22481, like so many other combat veterans, went to the 495th FTG at Atcham. The white bars and red surround to the National Insignia were introduced in mid-June 1943, but took some days to effect as the individual letters had to be repainted further aft on some aircraft. The profile shows the fighter equipped with a 108-US gallon metal tank attached to the 'belly' shackles.

12

P-47C-5 41-6326 of Lt Harold Comstock, 63rd FS, Halesworth, August 1943

One of the first P-47Cs received by the 56th, 41-6326 was issued to the 63rd FS on 28 January 1943. Assigned to Lt Harold Comstock, the aircraft was used by the future ace to shoot down two enemy aircraft and damage three others. Most of the group's original combat pilots changed to later P-47 models after a few months, although 'Bunny' Comstock preferred to keep his C because of its reliability, and the additional 'comforts' such as a cigarette lighter that crew chief Sgt Max Victor had installed. On the mission of 3 February 1944 the leader of B group extended duration to the limit, and several Thunderbolts were run very low on fuel. UN-Y was one of them, and it ran out soon after crossing the English coast, forcing Lt Comstock to belly in at Mutford. His beloved UN-Y hit a tree and came to rest somewhat demolished, but 'Bunny' was little harmed. The profile shows the P-47 equipped with a sheet steel 75-US gallon tank secured to the 'belly' shackles.

13

L-4B Grasshopper 43-686 of the 56th FG HQ, Halesworth, late summer 1943

Liaison aircraft for communication flights were scarce during the US Eighth Air Force's first 18 months in the UK, and several British types were used. The most popular aircraft for this role was the Piper L-4, commonly called Cub, and rarely by the USAAF official tag Grasshopper. L-4 43-686 saw only fleeting use with the 56th before being 'acquired' by a higher command. Later, the group received L-4B 43-666, which was given a red nose in 1944.

14

P-47D-5 42-8458 of Capt Francis Gabreski, 61st FS, Halesworth, September 1943

Capt Francis Gabreski's assigned P-47D-1-RE 42-7871 was initially coded HV-F, becoming HV-A when 'Gabby' received a new D-5 model in September 1943. The latter fighter duly became the new 'F for Francis', and Gabreski used it to shoot down three enemy aircraft in November. Whenever this P-47 was out of service, Gabreski would return to his old mount until, in late December 1943, this was in turn replaced with a new D-11. 42-8458/HV-F then became an unassigned aircraft, being used by a series of replacement pilots. It was slightly damaged in an abortive take-off accident at Halesworth whilst being flown by one of these new arrivals on New Year's Day 1944. Repaired, the veteran fighter was involved in yet another failed take-off just six days later, Lt Evan McMinn nosing the P-47 over. This time substantial damage was inflicted, and 42-8458 was unceremoniously scrapped. The profile shows the fighter equipped with the rarely-used Republic Aviation 200-US gallon 'paper' ferry tank, fitted flush to the aircraft's underfuselage. Just a handful of operational missions were flown using this store.

15

UC-61A Forwarder 43-14420, 56th FG HQ, Halesworth, September 1943

Just 12 of these popular Fairchild-built four-seat liaison aircraft initially reached the Eighth Air Force in April and May 1943, and these were quickly reserved for high command use. When more liaison types became available during the latter part of 1944, additional UC-61As were acquired by combat groups – the 56th FG HQ had 43-14420 for several months. However, even when at its most abundant in the ETO (in September 1944), there were only 27 UC-61s within the Eighth Air Force. The 56th painted the engine cowling on their Forwarder red in the summer of 1944.

16

P-47C-5 41-6343/*LITTLE COOKIE* of Capt Walter Cook, 62nd FS, Halesworth, October 1943

Capt Walter Cook scored four of his six victories in this P-47C-5, which was his assigned aircraft – it bore the name *LITTLE COOKIE* on both sides of the cowling. His remaining two kills (a pair of Fw 190s) were achieved on 11 November 1943 in P-47C-2 41-6193/LM-B, which he had been forced to use after *LITTLE COOKIE* suffered a flat tyre and subsequent propeller damage when landing on 20 October 1943. After repairs 41-6343 was retired to a training unit. Cook completed 66 missions before returning to the USA in February 1944.

17
P-47D-1 42-7938/"*HEWLETT-WOODMERE LONG ISLAND*" of Maj David Schilling, Deputy CO of the 56th FG, Halesworth, October 1943
Schilling's second assigned combat aircraft carried the dedication *"HEWLETT-WOODMERE LONG ISLAND"*, purchasers of War Bonds to the value of a P-47, on the left side of the fuselage. Schilling, one of the four pilots in the group to score in excess of 20 aerial kills, claimed three and one shared in this Thunderbolt, the first, an Fw 190, on 8 October 1943. In January 1944 Schilling took over a new D-11-RE model, and 42-7938 was passed to another pilot and the 'plane-in-squadron' letter changed from S to S. The aircraft ended its days with the 56th on 3 February 1944 when its pilot carried out a forced landing in a field after exhausting his fuel towards the end of a mission.

18
P-47C-2 41-6259 of Lt Glen Schiltz, 63rd FS, Halesworth, October 1943
This aircraft was assigned to Glen Schiltz from 8 February 1943 to 18 January 1944, when it was retired to Northern Ireland. The fighter later became a hack aircraft of the 65th FW, being based at Debden. Schiltz obtained five of his eight credited victories with this P-47, including his opening trio of kills (all Fw 190s) on 17 August 1943. On 11 January 1944 he was credited with a second triple-victory haul, although this time he was flying 41-6259's replacement, P-47D-11 42-75232/UN-Z.

19
P-47D-1 42-7877/"*JACKSON COUNTY*, MICHIGAN, FIGHTER"/IN THE MOOD of Capt Gerald Johnson, 61st FS, Halesworth, October 1943
A captain by the time he used this particular Thunderbolt to score 5.5 aerial victories, Gerald W Johnson was one of the 'Wolfpack's' most outstanding pilots. It was assigned to and flown by Gerry Johnson for his first confirmed victory on 26 June 1943 (an Fw 190), and he continued to use it until the end of 1943, although his final kill with the aircraft was scored on 14 October (another Fw 190). All Johnson's P-47s were 'razorbacks', and he achieved kills in at least five different aircraft.

20
P-47C-5 41-6325/'*Lucky Little Devil*' of Lt John Vogt, 63rd FS, Halesworth, October 1943
John Vogt was one of a number of VIII FC pilots who downed enemy aircraft while flying the same type of aircraft with more than one group – in his case the 56th and 356th FGs. The P-47C-5 depicted was his first assigned aircraft in the 56th, and he used it to score his first three victories. Vogt also flew a P-47D-20 and finally a D-25 'bubbletop' after transferring to the 360th FS/356th FG in late February 1944, the ace scoring his last three kills with this group for a final tally of 8-0-1. 41-6325 also transferred out of the 56th FG during the winter of 1944, leaving Halesworth in late January.

21
P-47C-2 41-6271/*Rat Racer* of Lt Frank McCauley, 61st FS, Halesworth, October 1943
One of the 56th FG's early aces, 'Mac' McCauley was assigned this P-47C-2, which he named *Rat Racer* – the words appear under the portrait of Mighty Mouse, just above the wing root. McCauley scored all of his 5.5 aerial kills in this aircraft, the P-47 exhibiting six victory symbols (one was later disallowed). After completing 46 missions, he left the 'Wolfpack' on 20 November 1943 and served out the war as an instructor with the 495th FTG.

22
P-47C-5 41-6347/*Torchy*/ "*LIL "AbNER*" of Capt Eugene O'Neill, 62nd FS, Halesworth, November 1943
Capt Gene O'Neill used this P-47C-5 to score his first 3.5 victories in November/December 1943 – the fraction was a Bf 110 he jointly shot down on 26 November 1943. The aircraft also carried a third name – *Jessie O* – on the starboard side adjacent to the cockpit. Having joined the 62nd PS in 23 December 1941, O'Neill used P-47D-10 42-75125/ LM-E to score his final kill on 6 February 1944. Although listed as an ace in numerous publications, both USAF Historical Study 85 and VIII Fighter Command Final Assessment credit him with 4.5 kills, having failed to find any record of that elusive fifth victory that would have made him an ace.

23
P-47D-11 42-75435/*Hollywood High Hatter* of Lt Paul Conger, 61st FS, Halesworth, December 1943
This grandly-named Thunderbolt was used by Paul Conger as a replacement for his originally assigned War Bond subscription P-47D-1 42-7880/HV-N "*REDONDO BEACH. CALIFORNIA*". The ace was almost certainly responsible for the three kills marked displayed under the cockpit of this fighter, which was subsequently transferred to the Boxted-based Air Sea Rescue Squadron in May 1944. Conger completed two tours with the 56th FG, completing the war flying P-47M-1 44-21134/UN-P. Like many other aces, Conger used at least three P-47s not assigned to him to reach his final tally of 11.5 kills.

24
P-47D-10 42-75163 of Lt Joe Powers, 61st FS, Halesworth, December 1943
Joe Powers received this aircraft as a replacement for C-2 41-6267/HV-V in early December 1943, having claimed single kills both in the former P-47 and C-5 41-6337/HV-S (both victims were Bf 109s). His first victories in the D-10, which he named *Powers Girl*, came on 11 December when he destroyed a Bf 109 and a Bf 110, and damaged a second *Zerstörer*. Powers subsequently flew a number of missions mostly in other P-47s (including 41-6267 yet again), although he did score kills in *Powers Girl* in January, February and March 1944. A captain by the time his tour ended in May 1944, Joe Powers' final tally was 14.5-0-5.

25
P-47D-11 42-75510 of Lt Col Francis Gabreski, CO of the 61st FS, Halesworth, January 1944
The first of two profiles (see also profile 28) of 'Gabby' Gabreski's P-47D-11 42-75510, this artwork shows the remarkably plain fighter whilst it was still adorned with standard VIII Fighter Command white recognition bands. Already his kill tally was beginning to steadily build up, the ace's score standing at eight victories at this point in his tour. 42-75510 was the third Republic fighter to be assigned to Gabreski following his arrival in the ETO in early 1943.

26
P-47D-5 42-8461/ "Lucky" of Lt Robert Johnson, 61st FS, Halesworth, February 1944

Robert S Johnson's third assigned aircraft, "Lucky" was used to score his third, fourth, fifth and sixth victories before being lost in the North Sea on 22 March 1944 with Dale Stream at the controls. Johnson had previously flown two C-model Thunderbolts, christened Half Pint and All Hell, and had shot down his first two kills in the latter aircraft, C-5 41-6235/HV-P. Following the loss of 42-8461, Johnson was assigned D-15 42-76234/HV-P.

27
P-47D-11 42-75242 of Capt Michael Quirk, 62nd FS, Halesworth, February 1944

Mike Quirk had used P-47C-2 41-6215/LM-K and D-2 42-22481/LM-J to score his first three kills prior to being assigned this P-47D-11. He went on to claim 6.5-1-1 in this aircraft, the last of which was downed on 25 February 1944 (an Fw 190). The Thunderbolt's overpainted tail band indicates a transition to coloured tactical markings, which this aircraft duly received while Quirk was still its regular pilot. He rose in rank to major on 17 September 1944, but by that time he had already been a PoW for a week after being downed by flak over Seligenstadt airfield on the 10th of the month. Quirk's final tally was 11-1-1.

28
P-47D-11 42-75510 of Lt Col Francis Gabreski, 61st FS, Halesworth, February 1944

Assigned to 'Gabby' Gabreski in December 1943 and used by him to shoot down ten of his 28 enemy aircraft, 42-75510 had its white theatre bands deleted in early February 1944 (see profile 25). The boss of the 61st FS replaced this aircraft with natural metal finish D-22-RE 42-25864, also coded HV-A, at the end of April. Crew chief S/Sgt Ralph Safford kept his aircraft in immaculate condition, making sure that they were always well polished. The 61st red nose band introduced early in February 1944 was later adopted as the group marking.

29
P-47D-11 42-75237/ WHACK!! of Lt Col Dave Schilling, Deputy CO of the 56th FG, Halesworth, February 1944

David Schilling's third LM-S replaced D-1 42-7938 in late January 1944. As with his previous fighters, the deputy CO had it adorned with another version of his favoured 'Hairless Joe' motif, which was a character from the Lil' Abner comic strip regularly featured in the Stars and Stripes service newspaper. WHACK!! was more an exclamation than a name for the Thunderbolt. As far as is known Schilling only shot down one enemy aircraft flying this P-47, but at least three more were claimed by other pilots who flew it. In May 1944, when Lt Col Schilling acquired another aircraft, 42-75237 became LM-S. Later, it was transferred to the 61st FS and brought down by flak on 5 September 1944, the pilot Lt Earl Hertel, evading capture.

30
P-47D-15 42-75864 of Col Hubert Zemke, CO of the 56th FG, Halesworth, March 1944

This modified P-47D-15RE was assigned to Col Hubert Zemke when he returned from the USA in January 1944.

The CO used this P-47 to obtain two-and-a-quarter victories (and a probable) over German fighters on 6 March 1944, and two days later Dave Schilling was flying it when he damaged an Fw 190. On 16 March the aircraft was completely destroyed when a fierce blaze broke out during a maintenance start-up at Halesworth.

31
P-47D-15 42-76179/ Little Chief of Lt Frank Klibbe, 61st FS, Halesworth, March 1944

Lt Frank Klibbe decorated at least two of his P-47s with a Red Indian head motif, complete with war bonnet and the wording Little Chief. This was the third Thunderbolt assigned to him, and he is believed to have scored four of his seven kills in it. Klibbe's missions with the 56th FG's 61st FS totalled 63.

32
P-47D-5 42-8487/" SPIRIT OF ATLANTIC CITY, N.J." of Capt Walker Mahurin, 63rd FS, Halesworth, March 1944

Capt 'Bud' Mahurin shot down a total of 19.75 aircraft, ranging from Fw 190s to a Ju 88, during his lengthy career with the 56th. This War Bond presentation aircraft (the second assigned to Mahurin) was used for all but three of these victories – the first two (Fw 190s) were achieved in C-2 41-6259/UN-V on 17 August, and he claimed a Bf 109 (and a second damaged) in D-11 42-75278/UN-B on 29 November. Unusual in that it retained its full squadron code letters (the inscription tended to replace the two letters on other subscriber-purchased P-47s), this machine is not known to have had any other form of personal marking on the starboard side. Mahurin was eventually shot down in it on 27 March 1944 by the rear gunner of a Do 217 that he helped destroy south of Chartres.

33
P-47D-6 42-74750/ Lady Jane of Lt John Truluck, 63rd FS, Halesworth, March 1944

John 'Lucky' Truluck scored his first kill in P-47D-1 42-7853/UN-R, before using the aircraft depicted here to score his second and third victories. He then enjoyed success with D-5 42-8488/UN-A on 26 November (an Fw 190 destroyed and a Bf 110 damaged) before reverting back to Lady Jane to 'make ace' on 24 February 1944 with an Fw 190 kill. Truluck claimed his sixth kill in D-10 42-75206/UN-G, although he again went back to Lady Jane to score his seventh, and final, victory (an Fw 190), plus a damaged (a Bf 109), on 15 March 1944.

34
P-47D-10 42-75207/ Rozzie Geth/ "BOCHE BUSTER" of Lt Fred Christensen, 62nd FS, Halesworth, March 1944

Although this aircraft was the first P-47 assigned to Fred Christensen, the 62nd FS's future ranking ace actually claimed his first of 21.5 kills in C-2 41-6193/LM-B. However, his next 10.5 victories were all downed in this D-10, which he continued to use until the late June 1944. Christensen flew a further two 'razorbacks' during his 107-mission tour.

35
P-47D-20 42-76234 of Capt Robert Johnson, 61st FS, late April 1944

This rather bland D-20 was Robert Johnson's assigned aircraft from late March to May 1944, when he transferred to the 62nd FS as a flight commander. Johnson shot down three enemy aircraft while flying this fighter, which has on occasion been erroneously referred to as *Double Lucky* – it did not carry any name or personal motif. 42-76234 was eventually salvaged by VIII Air Service Command in November 1944.

36
P-47D-21 42-25512/*Penrod and Sam* of Capt Robert Johnson, 62nd FS, Boxted, May 1944
Robert S Johnson's last P-47 was named for his groundcrew as a tribute to their outstanding work. Bob Johnson used up to four P-47s during his time in the ETO, one of which was lost whilst being flown by another pilot. This aircraft wore the ace's final score, which bettered that of World War 1 ace Eddie Rickenbacker by a single kill.

37
P-47D-22 42-26044/*Silver Lady* of Maj Leslie Smith, 61st FS, Boxted, May 1944
Although sven-kill ace Les Smith was assigned to fly this aircraft (one of the few unpainted P-47s in the 56th FG), it proved to be a successful talisman for such aces as 'Mike' Gladych and 'Gabby' Gabreski as well.

38
P-47D-26 42-28382/"*OLE COCK III*" of Capt Donavon Smith, 61st FS, Boxted, June 1944
Featured in two profiles (see also profile 43), Donavon Smith's last assigned Thunderbolt was his fourth of the tour. He made his final combat claim on 22 February 1944 against an Fw 190, bringing his overall total to 5.5-1-2, with a further two ground kills. Smith ended his duty as CO of the 61st FS on 10 January 1945, and this aircraft was transferred out of the 56th FG soon afterwards.

39
P-47D-22 42-26258 of the 63rd FS, Boxted, June 1944
This P-47 entered service with the 63rd FS in May 1944 and was lost on the following 5 September when pilot, 2Lt Chester Frye, was forced to bail out into captivity after the fighter was hit by flak fragments. At the time 42-26258 carried the slogan *Tops Mops Pride* on the fuselage. This aircraft was one of the few pre-bubble canopy P-47s within the 63rd FS to remain in natural metal finish.

40
P-47D-25 42-26628/*Rozzie Geth II/Miss Fire* of Capt Frederick Christensen, 62nd FS, Boxted, July 1944
Christensen accounted for kills 14 and 15 on 27 June (Bf 109) and 5 July 1944 (Fw 190) respectively in this aircraft, although his momentous haul of six Ju 52s in a single sortie was achieved on 7 July in D-21 42-25522/LM-H.

41
P-47D-22 42-26298/*Stalag Luft III/I Wanted Wings* of Lt Albert Knafelz, 62nd FS, Boxted, July 1944
A bare metal finish aircraft when first received at Boxted in early May 1944, 42-26298 was given a coat of Dark Green on its upper surfaces which was then over-sprayed with a disruptive pattern of Ocean Grey. The undersurfaces remained unpainted. Lt Albert Knafelz's second LM-A, he did not have to face the experience suggested by the unusual nose decoration.

42
P-38J Lightning 'Droop Snoot' of the 61st FS, Boxted, July 1944
A P-38 'Droop Snoot', coded CL-K, was transferred from the 55th FG in late July 1944 and assigned to the 61st FS. Removed to No 2 hangar at Boxted, it was given the 61st's colour markings and HV- codes. Only used on the fighter-bomber mission of 25 July 1944, the 'Droop Snoot' was severely damaged by flak and its pilot, none other than Col 'Hub' Zemke, made an emergency landing at Boxted. It is believed that the aircraft was subsequently salvaged.

43
P-47D-26 42-28382/"*OLE COCK III*" of Capt Donavon Smith, 61st FS, Boxted, August 1944
Donavon Smith's *OLE' COCK III* was received by the 61st FS in bare metal finish, although this had soon given way to the very distinctive camouflage and markings see here, and in profile 38. The upper surfaces were sprayed in a disruptive pattern of Dark Sea Grey and Light Sea Grey, this paint having been obtained from British sources. The undersurfaces were sprayed light blue – mostly likely Azure Blue. Apart from the usual red squadron colours, 42-28382 was the only camouflaged Thunderbolt at Boxted to have black code letters outlined in white.

44
P-47D-25 42-26413/"*OREGONS BRITANNIA*" of Col Hubert Zemke, CO of the 56th FG, Boxted, August 1944
Another aircraft depicted twice in the profile section (see profile 45), this Thunderbolt was the last example assigned to 'Hub' Zemke prior to his departure from the 56th to take command of the 479th FG on 12 August 1944. Bearing the War Bond inscription *"OREGONS BRITANNIA"*, it was used by Zemke to score six kills.

45
P-47D-25 42-26413/"*Oregons Britannia*"/*Happy Warrior* of Maj Harold E Comstock, CO of the 63rd FS, Boxted, September 1944
Following the 'Hub's' departure to the 479th, this aircraft was flown by five-victory ace Harold Comstock (and several other pilots), who had been CO of the 63rd FS since 19 July 1944. Comstock had the legend *HAPPY WARRIOR* added to the veteran fighter in celebration of his promotion to major on 17 September 1944. 42-26413 was finally written off when Lt Sam Batson stalled in after suffering an engine failure whilst on approach to landing at Boxted following a local flight. The pilot perished in the crash.

46
P-47D-25 42-26466/*ANAMOSA III* of Capt Russell Westfall, 63rd FS, Boxted, September 1944
Received by the 63rd FS in June 1944, 42-26466 was assigned to Capt Russell Westfall, who named it *ANAMOSA III*. Like most 'in-the-field' camouflaged P-47s of the 63rd FS, its upper surfaces were painted Dark Green, with the undersurfaces remaining in natural metal finish. Transferred out of the 56th early in 1945 following the arrival of P-47Ms at Boxted in the New Year, the aircraft duly went to the Ninth Air Force, where it was written off as salvage by the 48th FG at St Trond, in Belgium, in March.

47

P-47D-11 42-75276/CATEGORY "E" of the 63rd FS, Boxted, September 1944

This two-seat conversion P-47 had originally served as a single-seater within the 62nd FS as LM-M, completing 257 operational hours before retirement in August 1944. Delivered to the 56th in factory Olive Drab and Neutral Gray, the paint was removed from the airframe and a disruptive pattern of green and grey substituted in its place. The slogan "CATEGORY E" (which meant salvage status) was painted on the forward fuselage, although the aircraft was referred to as the 'Doublebolt' within the 56th. It was not written off as salvage until after VE-Day.

48

P-47M-1 44-21108 of Capt Witold Lanowski, 61st FS, Boxted, March 1945

Witold Lanowski was one of the Polish team that joined the 'Wolfpack' in the spring of 1944, and his tally of four kills made him the second most successful pilot of this small group behind 'Mike' Gladych. The nose emblem sums up the Poles' feeling towards the enemy – a factor that while living up to the aggressive spirit of the fighter pilot, tended to colour judgement in combat. The 61st FS had most of its P-47Ms camouflaged in this unconventional scheme by May 1945.

49

P-47D-28 44-19780/Teddy of Capt Michael Jackson, 62nd FS, Boxted, November 1944

Capt Michael Jackson was assigned 44-19780 in mid-September 1944, and he flew it until receiving a P-47M in February 1945 (see profile 52). Teddy entered service with a Dark Green and Light Sea Grey disruptive pattern on the upper surfaces, which was the commonest form of 'in-the-field' camouflage applied to 62nd FS aircraft. The undersurfaces remained in natural metal finish. Jackson, who scored five of his eight aerial victories in this aircraft, had both his air and ground strafing destroyed credits (5.5 in total) painted below the cockpit of Teddy – his aerial victories took the form of white outlined crosses.

50

P-47D-22 42-26299 of Capt Cameron Hart, 63rd FS, Boxted, September 1944

Typical of the rather beaten-up 'razorback' Thunderbolts that some elements of the 'Wolfpack' were still flying in late 1944, Cameron Hart's aircraft shows signs of wear and tear. Although four kills adorn this fighter, its assigned pilot only scored his first victory, a probable and a damaged (all Bf 109s on 5 September 1944) in this aircraft. The personal insignia has been attributed to a similar device carried by a Panzer unit – whatever its origins, Hart liked it, and carried it over into early October to his new mount, P-47D-28 44-19937/UN-B. He used the latter fighter to score four of his final tally of six kills. Remaining in the USAAF post-war, Cam Hart was killed in flying accident on 16 January 1946 when his P-47N (44-87929) crashed at Craig Field, Alabama.

51

P-47D-25 42-26641 of Col David Schilling, CO of the 56th FG, Boxted, December 1944

One of Dave Schilling's seven assigned P-47s, this fighter revealed an early 62nd FS penchant for painting Dogpatch cartoon characters on its Thunderbolts by featuring a neat rendering of 'Hairless Joe' on its cowling – although the name of the Al Capp character was not applied. Schilling's penultimate aircraft (he was issued with the 56th FG's first P-47M-1 in the form of 44-21125/LM-S just prior to leaving the group in January 1945), this D-25 was used by the colonel for his 'ace in a day' haul of five kills on 23 December 1944, which boosted his final tally to 22.5-0-6 – plus 10.5 ground kills. 42-26641 was declared war weary on 3 January 1945 after completing 55 combat sorties.

52

P-47M-1 44-21117/Teddy of Maj Michael Jackson, 62nd FS, Boxted, February 1945

Mike Jackson's P-47M probably shared much the same fate as other examples of the ultimate Thunderbolt variant to see action in the ETO – parked on a hardstanding at Boxted with engine cowling off and groundcrews setting about its troublesome engine. Jackson rounded out his total of eight confirmed aerial victories with a Bf 109 and an Fw 190D on 14 January 1945 flying P-47D-28 44-19780/LM-J. The extra kills marked on Teddy's scoreboard denote Jackson's 5.5 ground victories, hence their application in white.

53

P-47M-1 44-21114/MIM of Lt Col 'Pete' Dade, CO of the 56th FG, Boxted, March 1945

Initially the personal mount of group commanding officer, Lt Col 'Pete' Dade, 44-21114 was later re-assigned to Lt Fred Polansky. As with all operational P-47Ms of the 62nd FS, the aircraft had its upper surfaces camouflaged in a disruptive pattern of Dark Green and Light Sea Grey. Undersurfaces were unpainted and code letters and tail number were in Insignia Yellow. P-47Ms reaching the unit after VE-Day did not receive camouflage.

54

UC-64A Norseman 44-70239 of the 56th FG HQ, Boxted, April 1945

A popular Canadian-built liaison type, some 60 UC-64As were shipped to the UK in 1944. Norseman 44-70239 first came to Boxted to serve with the Air Sea Rescue Squadron, before later being transferred to the 56th FG HQ. Bare metal and silver doped on fabric surfaces, the aircraft's only unit marking was a red nose band. However, in May 1945 the code letters UN-L were painted under the left wing in black. Although assigned to group headquarters, the aircraft was serviced by the 63rd FS personnel, hence the codes.

55

P-47M-1 44-21212 of the 61st FS, Boxted, April 1945

Delivered to Boxted in January 1945 and painted up in the 61st FS's distinctive livery, 44-21212 was flown by a number of different pilots on the few operational missions in which it participated. The matt black colour on the upper surfaces of this squadron's aircraft had a decidedly purplish tinge.

56

P-47M-1 44-21112 of Maj George Bostwick, CO of the 63rd FS, Boxted, April 1945

George Bostwick spread his scoring from 7 June 1944 to 7 April 1945, ending the war with eight kills. Both his this aircraft and an earlier P-47D-22 (42-26289/LM-Z) assigned to him whilst still with the 62nd FS were referred to as 'Ugly Duckling', although the name was not painted on either aircraft. Bostwick was the only Thunderbolt ace to shoot down an Me 262, getting his jet on 25 March 1945 in M-1 44-21160/UN-F. He also damaged a second Me 262 in UN-Z on 7 April.

57

P-47M-1 44-21141/'*the Brat*' of Lt Randell Murphy, 63rd FS, Boxted, April 1945

Assigned to Lt Randell Murphy, this was the aircraft in which he claimed the destruction of ten enemy aircraft by strafing on 13 April 1945 – a record for one mission. It wears the standard 63rd FS camouflage for P-47Ms, namely a disruptive pattern of what is believed to be Dark Mediterranean Blue and Azure Blue on the upper surfaces,

with a sky blue rudder and tail number. The code letters were left as bare aluminium, and polished for silver sheen effect. Undersurfaces and wing leading edges remained unpainted.

58

He 111H-23 Wk-Nr 701152 of the 61st FS, Boxted, July 1945

A transport version of the stalwart Luftwaffe bomber was 'acquired' by senior offices of the 56th FG in July 1945 and painted up in the same 61st FS colour scheme that adorned its P-47Ms. The aircraft's groundcrew was headed by T/Sgt Barney Hunter, and they kept it in good flying order despite a complete lack of spare parts. Abandoned in September 1945 when the 56th finally returned to the USA, the Heinkel was retained by the RAF and eventually found its way into the RAF Museum at Hendon. Today, it is displayed in authentic Luftwaffe colours within the Battle of Britain Hall at this prestigious site.

UNIT HERALDRY

1

56th Fighter Group

The insignia of the 56th FG was devised while the group was training in the eastern United States, the emblem receiving official approval on 4 April 1942. It was expected that the group would eventually be equipped with P-38 Lightnings, hence the double lightning flash on the chevron. However, this served equally well to represent the Thunderbolt. The motto commonly used with this insignia during hostilities was *Ready and Waiting*, but at some point that officially approved was the Latin *Cave Tonitrum*, which translates as 'Beware of the Thunderbolt'.

2

61st Fighter Squadron

The approved 61st FS emblem features a caricatured English Bulldog's head with pilot's helmet and goggles. The lightning bolt clenched in its mouth represents the aircraft type flown, namely the P-47 Thunderbolt. The emblem was officially approved on 15 September 1943.

3

62nd Fighter Squadron

The emblem of the 62nd FS was inspired by a squadron pet bulldog. It features a cartoon version of the animal as a boxer wearing the colours of the *Stars and Stripes*. The device was officially approved on 18 June 1943.

4

63rd Fighter Squadron

The original emblem of the 63rd FS was a stylised device based on the shape of the P-38 Lightning, the fighter with which the squadron expected to be equipped in 1942. This was replaced by a caricatured pilot prostrate on a lightning bolt firing a machine gun. The lightning bolt represents the P-47 Thunderbolt, whilst the pilot was known unofficially within the unit as 'Gus the Gunner'. This emblem was the winning submission in a contest carried out at the Republic factory, which was judged by the then CO of the 63rd FS. The design was the work of a woman employed in the plant, and she received a prize of $50 for her efforts.

INDEX

Figures in **bold** refer to illustrations